The MYTH of CERTAINTY

*The Reflective Christian
and the Risk of Commitment*

The MYTH of CERTAINTY

*"We must know where to doubt,
where to feel certain, where to submit."*
—PASCAL

Daniel Taylor

JARRELL

A SPECIAL IMPRINT
OF
WORD BOOKS

THE MYTH OF CERTAINTY: THE REFLECTIVE CHRISTIAN
AND THE RISK OF COMMITMENT

Unless otherwise indicated, Scripture quotations are from *The New American
Standard Bible,* © The Lockman Foundation 1960, 1962, 1963, 1968, 1971,
1972, 1973, 1975, 1977.

Scripture quotations identified NEB are from *The New English Bible,* ©
1961, 1970 The Delegates of the Oxford University Press and The Syndics
of the Cambridge University Press.

Scripture quotations identified KJV are from the King James Version of
the Bible.

Bibliographic information for the chapter-opening epigraphs is listed in the
"Note" section.

Excerpts from the *Habit of Being* by Flannery O'Connor. Copyright ©
1979 by Regina O'Connor. Reprinted by permission of Farrar, Straus, and
Giroux, Inc.

Library of Congress Cataloging-in-Publication Data

Taylor, Daniel, 1948–
    The myth of certainty.

    Bibliography: p.
    1. Christian life—1960–   . I. Title.
BV4501.2.T274   1986   248.4   86–7176
ISBN 0–8499–0547–8

Printed in the United States of America

6 7 8 9 8   RRD   9 8 7 6 5 4 3 2 1

For my students—
in appreciation for my teachers

Contents

Introduction

What are you doing, you man, with the word of *God* upon *your* lips? Upon what grounds do you assume the role of mediator between heaven and earth? Who has authorized you to take your place there and to generate religious feeling?

—Karl Barth

These are not encouraging words. How can one justify more talk about God in an age that already talks too much and listens too little? Aren't there enough people in the church filling the air with many words and the shelves with glossy answers to all of life's questions? Do I not more readily identify with the young Moses who said, "Why me, Lord?" than with Isaiah's "Here am I, send me!"?

It's not the prospect of failure that is frightening. What, God forbid, if one should succeed? Imagine a dozen people believing whatever you tell them to believe; imagine a thousand, ten thousand, a countless following. How many times in the wilderness did Moses wonder if that burning bush had just been desert heatstroke?

Consider the television preacher and how fearfully he is made. I do not abuse him for being on television—it is the highest hill around. I do not complain that he asks for money— he has many barns to build. I allow him even his politics and prejudices (even as I wince when he makes them God's)

9

because I have my politics and prejudices as well. But I do stand amazed at one thing. Where, someone tell me, did he get this brimming confidence? Not his confidence before men and women—the psychology of that I can understand—but this confidence before God. Did *he* talk to a burning bush? Is he certain his sacrifice is not a stench in God's nostrils? Why are there no signs of ashes on his head? Why does he seem unconcerned with such questions? Even "send me" Isaiah despaired of his unclean lips.

And yet, there are reasons to speak, even a responsibility to do so. I am drawn to the spirit as well as the wisdom of Blaise Pascal, who over three hundred years ago gave a description of the human condition that is as timeless as it is eloquent:

> When I see the blindness and the wretchedness of man, when I regard the whole silent universe, and man without light, left to himself, and, as it were, lost in this corner of the universe, without knowing who has put him there, what he has come to do, what will become of him at death, and incapable of all knowledge, I become terrified. . . . And thereupon I wonder how people in a condition so wretched do not fall into despair. I see other persons around me of a like nature. I ask them if they are better informed than I am. They tell me they are not. And thereupon these wretched and lost beings, having looked around them, and seen some pleasing objects, have given and attached themselves to them. For my own part, I have not been able to attach myself to them, and, considering how strongly it appears that there is something else than what I see, I have examined whether this God has not left some sign of Himself.[1]

Here is cause enough to risk speaking. If there is no God, we are in desperate straits indeed. That fact alone is no proof that He must be, but it does place responsibility on those who have found signs of His presence. The lookout high up on the mast cries "Land ho" long before his foot can test whether it is land for certain. Those who have had glimpses of God must share them with anyone who is interested in listening.

This book, however, is not intended to convince anyone

to believe in God, or in the work of Christ, who does not believe already. It is not Christian apologetics in the usual sense. My direct concern is for those people who, like Pascal, have been unable to attach themselves to the world's "pleasing objects." They have found in God, and in Jesus Christ, a proposed solution to the human dilemma to which they have made, with varying degrees of confidence, a commitment. At the same time they have been blessed and cursed with minds that never rest. They are dissatisfied with superficial answers to difficult questions, willing to defend faith, but not its misuse.

Furthermore, these people find themselves in the church, members of a Christian subculture into which they were either born or later entered. Their relationship to this subculture is complex, and only partly conscious, and they are both indebted to it and victimized by it. At the same time, they are often part of, or heavily influenced by, another subculture which is basically indifferent or hostile to their Christian commitment. This is the secular, intellectual world that deals in the manufacture and propagation of ideas.

In writing to and for reflective Christians in these two subcultures, I am writing for myself, for this is where I spend my life. The problems addressed are, in many cases, ones I have or have had. Any advice given, I give myself, though I do not always heed it. My desire is to be of help, to make faith more possible not less, to lighten a burden not increase it, to write from the standpoint of faith but with open eyes and heart. I wish to talk with others who are also seeking signs of God in this world and desiring to act on what they have found. The false leads and illusions are many; the church is both part of the problem and part of the cure, but the goal is worth risking a life on.

I

The Nature of
Reflection

And pray to God to have mercy upon us
And I pray that I may forget
These matters that with myself I too much discuss
Too much explain
                                —*T. S. Eliot*

WHAT IS A REFLECTIVE CHRISTIAN, and why does it matter? Two very reasonable questions which I will attempt to answer soon. But first, let me ask *you* a few questions. Consider this a survey, a form of inquiry that has great appeal in our narcissistic and quasi-scientific age. (People are flattered to be asked what they think, and impressed with anything that can be turned into numbers.)

1. Are you, even after years of being a Christian, ever struck by the unlikelihood of the whole thing? Does one minute it seem perfectly natural and unquestionable that God exists and cares for the world, and the next moment uncommonly naive?

2. Do you ever think, "Those close to me would be shocked if they knew some of the doubts I have about my faith?" Do you ever scare even yourself with your doubts?

3. Have you sometimes felt like walking out of a church service because it seemed contrived and empty?

4. Have you ever felt intellectually embarrassed to admit that you were a Christian?

5. Do you ever feel somewhat schizophrenic about the relationship of your faith to the rest of your life? Do you find yourself compartmentalizing different aspects so that tensions between them are minimized?

6. If given a choice between sharing an island with Jerry Falwell and Phyllis Schlafly on the one hand, or Phil Donahue and Bella Abzug on the other, does one upset your stomach less than the other?

7. How often do you find yourself at odds with your surroundings—intellectually, socially, spiritually? Is there part of you which feels out of place no matter where you are?

8. On a controversial issue are you most likely to agree totally with one side, find all sides partially persuasive and attractive, or find yourself saying, "A plague on all your houses"?

9. Someone at work says, "Christians check their brains at the door of the church every Sunday, and most of them don't even bother to pick them up on the way out." Do you find yourself objecting or agreeing?

10. Someone at church says, "The humanists are destroying our country. We have got to elect Christian politicians and get this country back to God like it used to be." Are you more likely to say "Amen" or "Baloney"—or to grunt and change the subject?

11. How important is it for you to be certain about something before you act on it? Would you only invest money if there were no possibility for failure? Would you say "I love you" to someone before they had said it to you?

12. Do you consider yourself reasonable? Are you willing to take risks? Do you think of the two as contradictory?

13. Do you personally find a high degree of paradox in matters of faith, or does it seem primarily reasonable and logical?

14. How confident are you that you know God's desires regarding the specific political, social, and moral issues which face our society?

15. Would it bother you more to be thought a hypocrite or a cynic? Why?

16. Is it more immoral to act incorrectly in a significant situation or not to act at all?

There are, of course, no right or wrong answers to most of these questions. The pattern of your responses, however, may indicate the degree to which you are a reflective Christian.

The term *reflective Christian* brings to my mind a knot of related but quite different images. The first is very positive, evoking the simple wonder that among the things it means to be created in God's image is the ability to carry on a mental dialogue with reality—that is, to think.

It evokes also, in this regard, that long tradition of people of faith who have valued and participated in the life of the mind and who have brought their God-given intelligence and imagination to bear on the society in which they have lived.

These believers have been involved thoughtfully in their cultures, sometimes as shapers, sometimes as critics, but always as people who thought the human endeavor worthwhile.

But there is also a more troublesome aspect to being reflective. Thinking, as many have discovered, can be dangerous. It can get us in trouble—with others, but also with ourselves. And the suspicion lingers in religious circles that it can also, if we are not very careful, get us in trouble with God.

It is on these different notions of the term *reflective Christian* that I wish to focus. What are the perils and opportunities of being a thinking Christian in the late twentieth century? How does one survive as a thinker in the church and as a believer in the larger world? And can one do any more than "survive"; can one be the arms and eyes and voice of God to our society in the same way that earlier reflective Christians were to theirs?

A DISCUSSION OF TERMS

The reflective person is, first and foremost, a question asker—one who finds in every experience and assertion something that requires further investigation. He or she is a stone-turner, attracted to the creepy-crawly things that live under rocks and behind human pronouncements. The writer of Ecclesiastes was such a person: "I directed my mind to know, to investigate, and to seek wisdom and an explanation . . ." (Eccles. 7:25, NASB).

To be reflective is to be sensitive to and fascinated by the complexity of things. It entails an openness to the nuances and grace notes of life, and it implies an eye for hidden beauties and white-washed sepulchers. The reflective person seeks demarcation in the indivisible and finds unity in diversity, discovering likeness in seemingly unlike things.

True reflection leads one, like the writer of Ecclesiastes, toward ultimate questions. A person with endless curiosity about the physical workings of the world, or of political and social structures, or of human psychology, who does not ask with any urgency, "Why am I here?" is not, to my mind, genuinely reflective. Reflection often leads one to the questions traditionally addressed by religion, though it will not necessarily be satisfied with religion's varying answers.

Reflectiveness should not be confused with the amassing of information, nor with intelligence. Many with great stores of knowledge, intellect, and unquestionable expertise are not particularly reflective. Some who are very reflective, on the other hand, are ill-informed, not strongly logical, perhaps not even especially bright.

Clearly it is a matter of degree. Everyone reflects to some extent, including many who are mentally retarded. For some, however, reflection sets the tone for their lives in ways that bring both pleasure and pain. Looking under rocks has its disadvantages.

I remember well my own early struggles with faith and doubt as a college student. What stands out most clearly is the paradoxical combination of constant motion and paralysis. My mind was constantly moving, but my will was paralyzed. A great sense of the wonder and complexity and challenge of being human was the gift of my growing reflectiveness (and the priceless legacy passed on to me by my teachers). The cost was an ever diminishing ability to say, "This is true, that is not; this is good, that is evil; this I will do, that should not be done."

Reflection counseled me never to commit. It said, "This may seem true to you now, but what about tomorrow? Don't you think you should know more? Is there something you aren't considering? Hadn't we better wait on this? There are others who see things differently, you know." This line of questioning is, of course, the orthodoxy of our day, not least because it has a genuine basis in truth. (But what, the voice says, *is* truth anyway?)

Because my mind sought answers ceaselessly to the important questions in life but at the same time rejected all answers to those questions, and almost even the possibility of answers,

I was a prime candidate for misery and cynicism. And superficially cynical I was, and miserable I might have been, but for my congenitally easy-going attitude toward life.

Reflectiveness, then, is a character trait deeply rooted in what one essentially is. It helps define one's fundamental experience of reality. The life of a reflective person is more likely to be interesting, less likely to be serene; more likely to be contemplative, less likely to be active; more likely to be marked by the pursuit of answers, less by the finding of them. The result is a high potential for creativity, curiosity, and discovery, but also for paralyzing ambivalence, alienation, and melancholy.

I see this doubleness frequently in the experience of my students, not to mention in myself. Oh, how alive the thinking and feeling ones are! Alive to the new-found pleasures of the mind, of ideas contemplated, poked at, then swallowed whole to become in some unique way part of them—sometimes for fifteen minutes, sometimes forever. But they are alive also to the pain of thought, to the sometimes agonizing attempt to reconcile the inner world with the outer one.

One bright young woman expressed to me a whimsical desire for the simple, naive view of life she once had as an active member of her church's high school youth group. But with a quiet earnestness she observed, "I can't unlearn what I've learned since then." No, she can't, though she may learn enough in the future to discover that while a little learning alienates, much learning often reconciles.

Being reflective is both a blessing and a curse, a potential for strength and for weakness. It can lead equally well toward truth or error. Life can be richer, more textured, more challenging, more meaningful. Likewise, it can become more barren, more threatening, more overwhelming.

Reflection can awaken one to the possibilities of life and the need for involvement. More typically, however, it leads away from whole-hearted engagement. Awareness of the multiplicity of choices, the infinitude of implications, the tension of competing claims, the constant possibility for error, all coupled with the desire to act correctly, militates against the "I choose this" of commitment.

Hamlet is the archetype of this aspect of the reflective personality. Act he must; act he cannot. For him, as for many like him, "the native hue of resolution / Is sicklied o'er with the pale cast of thought." His many modern literary counterparts are found in the works of writers like T. S. Eliot and Samuel Beckett, compulsively introspective characters whose minds grind on endlessly but whose wills are frozen.

Reflection in this sense is the nearest human realization of perpetual motion. It is insatiable. It is hostile to the notion of conclusion. The questioning mind is a dictator satisfied with nothing less than a thousand-year reign. Why should it stop? Why relinquish its hold? It is inherent in the very nature of reflection to resist limitation. The more one tries to restrict it, the more power one gives it; for reflection is suspicious of nothing so much as attempts to quell it. It may lie low for a time, but will blaze back all the fiercer for having been suppressed.

The ceaselessness of reflection works both for good and for ill, but in either case it is often exhausting. Everyone needs relief from the potentially endless cycle of assertion, analysis, counterassertion, qualification, redefinition, exceptions, extenuations, complications, hidden presuppositions, emotional colorings, summations, ad infinitum.

Gerard Manley Hopkins felt something of this when he wrote the following:

> My own heart let me more have pity on; let
> Me live to my sad self hereafter kind,
> Charitable; not live this tormented mind
> With this tormented mind tormenting yet. . . .
>
> Soul, self; come poor Jackself, I do advise
> You, jaded, let be; call off thoughts awhile. . . .[1]

Who has not felt at times the overwhelming desire to "call off thoughts awhile"? Our reflective powers, one of our greatest gifts, can become our greatest curse. No dripping faucet was ever as maddening as the steady beat of a mind going in circles, chained to a problem which admitted neither solution nor capitulation.

I find all around me wounded people of all ages and varied backgrounds—friends, acquaintances, a few who tell me of their struggles, more about whom I conjecture. Some struggle over the possibilities of faith in a faithless world, others with their relationship to the church and their own distorted upbringings, still others with their place in the secular marketplace. Many of these people drift in limbo, often confused, sometimes discouraged, frequently hurt.

Some make the best of it, chalk it up to "the way life is," push ahead with plucky resolve, find a way to survive, make do, get along. . . . Others cope less well. For them there is no middle ground. At times they are more honest than the rest of us, other times only more confused. They break up, often quietly, and drop away. Sometimes they lash out; sometimes they settle into a kind of subdued schizophrenia.

Usually in my experience these are the reflective ones—not that this is a *necessary* result of being reflective, but that reflection is a quality which makes one more susceptible to certain kinds of wounds. I believe that something can be done. I am no fan of quick fixes, spiritual or otherwise, but I do believe we are at a historically crucial time in the life of the Christian church and human society. Reflective Christians are, as they have always been, a great gift from God with important tasks to do. They cannot do them if mired in endless cycles of reflection without action. They also cannot do them, however, if they forfeit the life of the mind for mindless parroting of simplistic, culturally determined socio-religious agendas.

My hope is that better understanding the subcultures in which the reflective Christian often lives, and seeing clearly *one* view of faith to which some Christians are called, will make more possible a commitment to a life of faith and risk and action that both the church and the world greatly need.

SUBCULTURES AND THE PSYCHOLOGY OF BELIEF

Every person, whether reflective or not, has a way of making sense out of the world. It is as fundamental a need as eating and breathing (and comes far ahead of sex). We have a compulsion for ordering and explaining our experiences, even if we decide that the governing principle of life is disorder. (Asserting that life is chaotic or absurd is simply one way of explaining— giving order to—one's experiences.)

But we do not make sense out of the world all by ourselves. We do so in the context of other people trying to do the same thing. This is one way of defining subcultures, those smaller groupings of people sharing something in common. Each of us participates in a variety of different subcultures at the same time, some of which can be defined broadly—caucasian, middle class, American. Others are defined very narrowly—antique collectors, Klu Klux Klanners, detective novel devotees.

We belong to communities of belief which help shape, whether we are conscious of it or not, our views of the world and our actions in it. We both draw from these communities and contribute to them, the reflective and the unreflective alike. They help determine what we are.

I want to focus my attention on two of these subcultures because I think they do the most to shape the life of the reflective Christian. The first is the *Christian subculture,* particularly the more conservative wing of western Christendom. Since I am writing largely from my own experience, I will take my examples from that part of the church that calls itself "evangelical," or, with different connotations, "fundamentalist," though I believe what I have to say about risk and commitment are important for those who have no contact with this one branch of God's work.

The second subculture, even less precisely definable than the first, is the secular marketplace, especially the marketplace of ideas. If tremendous diversity exists within Christendom, there is even more within what I have chosen to call *the secular, intellectual subculture.* For our purposes, it is that part of our secular culture which trades in ideas—the makers and consumers of education, books, films, plays, art, opinion, popular thought, and so on. It includes but is not limited to the academic world of scholarship and higher education, and many so-called "secular humanists" (the current boogeymen for parts of conservative Christendom).

Both these subcultures greatly influence the typical reflective Christian. They are the source of much that is good in their lives, but also of much of the pain, tension, and unfocused anxiety. Understanding something of how these subcultures relate to those within their spheres of influence, and to each other, can be freeing.

Before looking at these subcultures in particular, however, it is helpful to consider the psychology of belief in general. Understanding something of not *what* people believe, but *why* and *how* they believe can protect one from self-created illusions and from manipulation by both of these subcultures.

An awareness of the psychology of belief will also help conserve energy. When in tension with one's surroundings, it is valuable to understand that some battles, even losing ones, are worth fighting, but that others are a waste of resources. Recognizing the difference can save one's energy for more profitable efforts.

Human beings are explanation generators. We crave explanation because it contributes to perhaps the most basic of all nonphysical human needs—the need for security. From our earliest moment to our last we are vulnerable. Destruction—physical, mental, emotional, spiritual—threatens us at all times. A fall from a curb, a lost job, a bitter word, a public humiliation—at every point we feel the hazards of life. The great bulk of human activity of every kind aims at lessening that vulnerability. Making money, seeking love or accomplishment, buying insurance, courting power, wearing the right shoes, writing books, having children, reading books, not having children, not reading books—all these and countless other daily activities are ways of protecting ourselves from the myriad threats to our sense of personal safety and well-being.

The ways of making sense of our existence that we generate as a response to our essential fragility are among the most powerful things in the world. The less conscious they are the more powerful, and much will be unconscious even to the most introspective. Most people thoughtlessly adapt an inherited world view, or one absorbed from their surroundings. Even those who explicitly work one out often operate in daily life by a different, less conscious system than the one they carefully construct.

Why do we believe what we believe? Epistemological relativists and social scientists have a field day with such questions, rattling on confidently about psychological needs, social conditioning, and even genetics. Conservative Christian apologists like the question less, being much more comfortable with "what" than "why" in regards to belief. Their response is likely to be a simple "Because it's true" or "Because the Bible says so" regarding their own beliefs, and "Because people are sinful" when dealing with opposing alternatives.

We believe what we do about the world, of course, for many different reasons. All ways of explaining the world tend to be self-verifying and self-sustaining. An outlook does not have to be "right" in order to seem right. It need not be logical (though most people will consider their position reasonable), nor consistent, nor thorough, nor defendable, nor anything else to fulfill its primary function—providing an explanation of things. Once in operation, a belief system processes all information, all evidence, in its own terms, appropriating that which verifies its outlook and defusing or ignoring anything else.

The foregoing is much more true for the typical person than it is for the very reflective. The latter tend not only to open their view to serious question, but to allow the irresistible reflecting process to devour their own views along with all others.

For the reflective and unreflective alike, however, world views persist because they work. Even the most repulsive or bizarre approaches to life succeed in the essential task of providing a way of processing experience, and often have other benefits as well. Nazism made sense to those who practiced it and brought a false feeling of worth to a discouraged people. Drug addicts, alcoholics, and punk rockers all have "reasons" why they are what they are. Even the choice to end life may seem sensible to one looking to relieve personal suffering.

It is no wonder, then, that world views are not easily changed. From a limited perspective they all work, allowing their adherents to at least function in a threatening world. The *ultimate* value of an approach to life, of course, requires higher criteria and a broader context of judgment. The view from eternity is, finally, the telling one, though that is a glass in which we see darkly.

Whatever the world view, it must deal with opposition. No belief system is comfortable with competing systems, not even those which explicitly claim to be. At the deepest level, difference threatens. It challenges our sense of security. Only a great deal of conditioning can partly overcome this sense of danger.

Most educated people today pride themselves on their tolerance. The great majority would call themselves pluralists, believing there are many different and equally valid ways of explaining the world and solving its problems. Even the most ardent pluralist, however, appears tolerant of many different outlooks only because they are *allowed for* in his or her point of view.

The pluralist expects to find many different perspectives in the world and does so, thereby confirming his or her outlook. He or she is likely to feel offended, even threatened, however, by the person who claims there is only a single correct explanation of reality or a single right answer to a social problem. As the current wailings of doctrinaire pluralists about the political and social activities of the *new right* in America demonstrate, most pluralists are no more tolerant of *truly* divergent points of view than those they criticize for intolerance.

Every belief system repels competitors in a variety of ways. These include ignoring their existence, belittling and caricaturing the enemy to make it unattractive, considering only selective evidence, threatening dissenters within one's own group, appealing to tradition, ostracizing, and so on. Similar tactics are used to defend very different points of view. Receiving mail from both ends of the socio-political spectrum, I am amazed at the similarity of the charges they make against each other (violating basic human rights, haters of the good and the true, a threat to the American way of life, part of a greater conspiracy, and so on), and the almost identical tactics of fear and scorn they use. Each is immune to the arguments of the other, finding in them only further confirmation of their own position.

We fend off competing world views because by threatening our present understanding of reality they threaten our essential security. An unbeliever presented with the claims of God, for instance, or a believer confronted with the view that God is mere wish-fulfillment are both being told that any meaning and security they have derived from their explanation of the world is spurious and illusory. Confronted with radical disorientation, the initial response is to preserve the self and the status quo. Flannery O'Connor realized this when she wrote in one of her letters, "my communications . . . sound as if they came from a besieged defender of the faith. I know well enough that it is not a defense of the faith, which don't need it, but a defense of myself who does." [2]

When people defend their world view, they are not defending reason, or God, or an abstract system; they are defending their own fragile sense of security and self-respect. It is as instinctive as defending one's body from attack. No one understood the psychology of this better than Kierkegaard. He recognized how subtly intertwined are our beliefs with our instinct for self-preservation, and counseled the greatest sensitivity for those who seek to lead someone from error into truth:

> First and foremost, no impatience. . . . A direct attack only strengthens a person in his illusion, and at the same time embitters him. There is nothing that requires such gentle handling as an illusion, if one wishes to dispel it. If anything prompts the prospec-

tive captive to set his will in opposition, all is lost. . . . [T]he indirect method . . . , loving and serving the truth, arranges everything . . . , and then shyly withdraws (for love is always shy), so as not to witness the admission which he makes to himself alone before God—that he has lived hitherto in an illusion.[3]

How far this wise, compassionate approach is from the battering ram, take-no-prisoners attitude of many contemporary apologists for various causes. Only those with great confidence in the truth they hold can risk Kierkegaard's approach. The less secure must annihilate the opposition.

Given the nature of belief, it is no wonder that the reflective Christian will attract the displeasure of any subculture in which he or she is perceived as a threat to the ruling orthodoxy. Though they may be treated with derision or condescension, they are fundamentally frightening. And fear, Jacques Ellul observes, "dictates two modes of behavior: violence and rigidity." [4] Violence takes various forms, most often verbal or attitudinal in the two subcultures we are considering. Rigidity arises from the attempt to achieve stability (security) through paralysis—if nothing changes, then everything will be all right. (Such rigidity is part of the popular caricature of the conservative, but how often do people of any stripe admit fundamental error in their view of things?)

Why all this on the psychology of belief? Because it helps to discover you may not be crazy. If you get out of step in a subculture you are often subtly made to feel if not crazy, then guilty, or stupid, or anything else that will pressure you back into the pack. And these feelings heighten if you assume that everyone else believes what they do for unimpeachable reasons, while your difficulties merely evidence your own weakness, recalcitrance, or bad manners.

Sometimes that may be the case, but often reflective people are out of step because they sense that something is not right. They may be confused themselves, but they should be listened to. God has often used those with troubled hearts to speak to their society and to call His people closer to Himself.

2
The Reflective Christian and the Church

Men never do evil so completely and cheerfully as when they do it from religious conviction.
—Pascal

People are leaving the churches and returning to God.
—Lenny Bruce

I ONCE ASSIGNED A CLASS to read a book which dealt with the loss a young Mexican-American boy felt when his learning English alienated him from the protective intimacy of his Spanish-speaking family. A man in his forties wrote the following response in his class journal:

> I thought of the struggle I have had as I read and as new things became more important. Reading theology was more important than my job, than my family at times. I would lock myself in my room and read. The more I read the harder it was to communicate with my wife about things of the Lord. The old friends I had—I know they thought that I was backsliding in my faith. I read so much and such thought-expanding books that at times my head hurt like something inside was trying to get out. I kept telling myself, and at times I still do, that I wouldn't read any more theology—only the Bible. At times I felt like Jeremiah in his work: "When I say I will not speak in His name, there is like a fire within and I cannot contain it." Still . . . there is a loss. At times, I would like to go back but I can't—there is no way to retreat.

One could not hope for a more eloquent statement of the dilemma of the reflective Christian within the church. Why did reading theology make it more difficult for this man to talk about spiritual things to his wife? Why did reading and thinking become more important than earning money or his relationship with others? Why did it cause his friends to think he wasn't as good a Christian as he had been before? What was it inside him that was trying to "get out"? What does he mean by "there was a loss"? What is it he sometimes wants to "go back" to, and why can't he?

This passage illustrates a tension many feel within the Christian subculture. The church, it seems, is not comfortable with a whole complex of related behaviors that, for better or worse, often characterize the reflective Christian. These include asking real questions, probing standardized answers, going through

periods of strained belief or unbelief, being angry or disillu-
sioned—sometimes with God—and generally not behaving in
the accepted fashion.

Many reflective Christians, I hasten to point out, have a
positive and mutually supportive relationship with the church
and the subculture. It is ridiculous to suggest that anyone
who thinks must necessarily be at odds with fellow believers.
I am writing, however, for a large minority who find life within
the church more difficult. Where some find comfort and acceptance, others also find criticism and rejection. Where many
find freedom and the opportunity for service and growth, others
find restriction and the denial of their gifts. Both the individual
and the church contribute to this situation, and both can contribute to its healing.

It is simultaneously the blessing and the curse of the reflective
Christian that believers are called to live out their faith in
the church. No institution has accomplished so much for good
in the world; none has fallen so short of its calling! The church
is God-ordained, God-inspired, but accomplishes its work
through human beings subject to every possible failing.

Because it takes so many different forms in the world, one
cannot speak of "the church" as though it were even remotely
a single entity with a consistent set of attitudes and outlooks.
And yet there are recurring patterns in the experience of the
thinking Christian within this subculture.

Above all, Christians who find themselves in conflict with
the church should recognize that the church is, at the very
same time, both a divine and a human institution. The church
does not like thinking of itself as an institution, certainly not
in the same sense as all other human institutions. It prefers
the New Testament metaphors of the church as the body of
Christ—an organism not an organization—or as Christ's bride,
or as the communion of saints. Certainly these are the goals
of the church, realized here and there, now and then. The
parallel reality, however, is that at the same time the church
is an institution which operates, consciously or not, like other
human institutions.

The primary goal of all institutions and subcultures is

self-preservation. Preserving the faith is central to God's plan for human history; preserving particular religious institutions is not. Do not expect those who run the institutions to be sensitive to the difference. God needs no particular person, church, denomination, creed, or organization to accomplish His purpose. He will make use of those, in all their diversity, who are ready to be used, but will leave to themselves those who labor for their own ends.

Nonetheless, questioning the institution is synonymous, for many, with attacking God—something not long to be tolerated. Supposedly they are protecting God, an almost humorous notion if its consequences were not so hurtful. Apparently God is fragile, His feelings easily hurt, sort of like Mr. Snuffleupagus on "Sesame Street" who feels sad and frustrated when people don't believe he exists. Actually, they are protecting themselves, their view of the world, and their sense of security. The religious institution has given them meaning, a sense of purpose, and, in some cases, careers. Anyone perceived as a threat to these things is a threat indeed.

This threat is often met, or suppressed before it even arises, with power. All institutions and subcultures have power. It is granted by its members and is exercised in many ways for various purposes. There is nothing inherently good or evil in this situation. Power can be exercised for benefit or harm, and many of its uses in the Christian subculture are legitimate and beneficial. Power is so easily misused, however, that even the most sincere often exercise it improperly.

Institutions express their power most clearly by enunciating, interpreting, and enforcing the rules of the subculture. Every institution has its rules and ways of enforcing them, some clearly stated, others unstated but no less real. Rules are necessary and for the most part, like power, morally neutral in principle. The unique feature of religious institutions is the claim that their rules come from God. (Secular institutions often appeal to a similarly transcendent source—tradition, reason, the will of the people, and so on.)

To varying degrees, the believer accepts this claim. It is

painfully clear, however, to anyone who has a passing acquaintance with church history, past and present, that much of what passes for God's word and God's way is man's word and man's way. Churches, *at the same time* that they are aspects of God's plan for human history, are also sociological, culturally conditioned, human institutions.

We need not lament this fact, but we should recognize it. Christianity is, above all others, a historical faith that takes place amidst human institutions. That modern American Christianity reflects many different strains of modern American culture is inevitable. No culturally free church (or theology) has ever existed or ever should. (Certainly, those who presently cry loudest in the church about the infection of secular culture are among the most infected—typically by American materialism, hype, and chauvinist politics.) While the influence of culture is inevitable, we should be unsparingly self-critical about those places where that influence dilutes or distorts the perfect will of God.

(In order to explore these issues in another medium and to provide some relief from page after page of exposition, I will offer for your contemplation from time to time in this book the adventures and misadventures of one particular reflective Christian by the name of Alex Adamson.)

* * * * *

Even the knock gave him away. It was rapid but weak, as though the door was hot and he was afraid of burning his knuckles. The Dean entered the office at Alex's invitation and was too jovial from the start.

"A nice big office you have here, Alex. Can you see the lake from here?"

Alex was not one to let a man splash around helplessly. He offered what support he could.

"Well, I guess I could see the lake if there weren't so many trees in the way. Maybe it'll be more visible in the winter."

"This is your first year here at Redeemed, isn't it, Alex?"

This wasn't splashing around; it was drowning. Of course it was his first year here. The Dean himself had hired him only a few months earlier. But maybe this was the Dean's transition to the reason for his visit, the first they'd had since the job interview. Alex decided to keep up his end of the conversation.

"Yes."

"Well, that's right. It is your first year here. And it takes awhile for anyone from the outside to learn how to fit into a new situation, to learn to be part of the family you might say."

This was ominous.

"Now we've been very pleased with your work so far . . ."

The kiss of death. That's what they said right before firing baseball managers. Alex ran through a quick mental checklist. He'd worn a coat and tie every day as per the President's memo.

". . . and there's really no cause for concern . . ."

It's getting worse. As best he could remember, he had kept the door of his office open when speaking with female students, and had not sat on the desk in the classroom when lecturing—two points the President had emphasized in his remarks to the faculty before the start of the term.

". . . you've got a great future here at Redeemed."

Chapel! It must be that day he missed chapel last week. He knew the Dean slipped into the little balcony at the back with the organ pipes and checked on faculty chapel attendance—an old-timer had let him in on that trick—but he didn't think one miss would mean much.

"I'm having a little trouble here getting right to the point."

"I think I know what you have in mind, Dean."

"Good, then you won't mind printing a retraction?"

A retraction?

"A retraction?"

"Well, maybe you're right. A retraction would only call attention to the whole thing. I'll stand by you there, Alex. I'll tell the President there won't be any retraction, but that he won't have to worry about this kind of thing again."

"I'm sorry, Dean. You're going to have to start from the beginning. What are you talking about?"

"The article you wrote in the student newspaper attacking Professor Shell."

Alex was stunned. He saw instantly the depth of his own naiveté. He had known that going from graduate school to Redeemed College would be changing worlds, but he now saw they scarcely obeyed the same laws of time and space.

"I didn't 'attack' Dr. Shell. I merely disagreed with him."

"Same thing."

"Not at all the same thing. He wrote an article for the paper on the proper Christian attitude toward existentialism. I didn't agree with his conclusions, so I wrote a response."

The Dean kept a sympathetic look on his face while Alex spoke, his slight smile a sturdy defense against alien opinions.

"You know the Bible says that if we have ought against our brother we should go to him, first alone, and then with witnesses. Did you try to work this out with Dr. Shell?"

Alex was almost paralyzed by the incongruity of the Dean's words. The Dean was known for having raised *nonsequitur* to an art form, and Alex searched futilely for the missing link.

"I don't have ought . . . anything against Dr. Shell. I simply have a different point of view, one I thought the students would profit from hearing. If I go talk to Dr. Shell, that doesn't help them see that maybe there is more than one way of thinking about something like existentialism, about everything for that matter."

"Everything, Alex?" The Dean raised one eyebrow.

It was a nightmare. At this point on television the accused would snap that he wasn't saying anything else until he talked to his lawyer. Somehow that line didn't seem right for this situation.

"All I'm saying is that I thought this is one of the things a student newspaper was for, a place for people to air their opinions, give and take on various issues. Isn't that right?"

"In a sense, Alex, in a sense. It depends, though, on what people's opinions are. Opinions can be very dangerous. Students can be misled and their parents upset by the wrong kind of opinions. Fortunately, as Christians we have the Word of God and don't have to rely on people's opinions of things."

"But we're talking about the student paper, not the Bible."

By this time the Dean had taken on a very fatherly air. His earlier nervousness had vanished.

"The Bible has to do with everything, including the student paper. The Bible tells us that a doubter is unstable in all his ways. Dissension among faculty members in front of students produces doubt, and you know where that leads as well as I do."

Alex didn't know but was too confused to inquire. How could you carry on a reasonable discussion with such Hydra-headed illogic? Every misconception vanquished generated two more in its place. Alex sat mute in numb defeat.

"Now I don't want this to upset you, Alex. No one is angry. The President just thought I should help you get settled in a little quicker here at Redeemed. I'll let him know that we had a good talk."

The Dean sidled over to the door as he spoke. After opening it he stopped and looked back.

"You might want to drop a short note to Dr. Shell, though. Or maybe buy him a cup of coffee. I think his feelings might be hurt a little, but he's not one to hold a grudge. Don't worry."

The click of the closing door sounded like a trigger pulled on an empty chamber.

*　*　*　*　*

The danger toward which the appropriate exercise of authority always tends is authoritarianism—the exercise of authority for its own sake and to ensure its own perpetuation. The great weapon of authoritarianism, secular or religious, is legalism: the manufacturing and manipulation of rules for the purpose of illegitimate control. Perhaps the most damaging of all the perversions of God's will and Christ's work, legalism clings to law at the expense of grace, to the letter in place of the spirit.

Legalism is one more expression of the human compulsion for security. If we can vigorously enforce an exhaustive list of dos and don'ts (with an emphasis on external behavior), we not only can control unpredictable human beings but have God's favor as well. Jacques Ellul's description of a kind of pseudo-faith always prevalent in Christendom casts light on the attitude of the legalist:

> They comply unfailingly with the law and the commandments. They are unbending in their convictions, intolerant of any deviation. In the articulation of belief they press rigor and absolutism to their limits. They precisely delimit the frontiers between believers and unbelievers. They unceasingly refine the expression of their belief and seek to give it explicit intellectual formulation in a system as coherent and complete as possible. They insist on total orthodoxy. Ways of thinking and acting are rigidly codified.[1]

None of us, of course, recognizes ourself here, only someone else. But we should all recognize the extent to which we, like the legalist, want to tame God and the claims He makes so as to keep our lives safer, neater, and under our own control.

Legalistic authoritarianism shows itself in the confusion of the Christian principle of unity with a human insistence on unanimity. Unity is a profound, even mystical quality. It takes great effort to achieve, yet mere effort will never produce it; it is a source of great security, yet demands great risk.

Unanimity, on the other hand, is very tidy. It can be measured, monitored, and enforced. It is largely external, whereas unity is essentially internal. Its primary goal is correct behavior, while unity's is a right spirit. Unanimity insists on many orthodoxies in addition to those of belief and behavior, including orthodoxy of experience and vocabulary. That is, believers are expected to come to God in similar ways, to have similar experiences with God, and to use accepted phrases in describing those experiences. Flannery O'Connor recognized the danger of the latter when she wrote, "I try militantly never to be affected by the pious language of the faithful but it is always coming out when you least expect it," adding later, "I doubtless hate pious language . . . because I believe the realities it hides." [2]

The passing remark of a friend of mine illustrates in a small way the great price the church, as well as the individual, pays because of this often unconscious expectation of unanimity. He had turned down a request to teach an adult Sunday school class. "I don't want to go through the hassle that comes when I give my answers to the questions that come up. I have tried teaching in the past and someone always gets upset. It just isn't worth it." How much does the church lose of the gifts and enthusiasm of its members because it creates an atmosphere where honesty and risk are not welcomed?

Only the most extreme elements of Christendom actually insist on thorough uniformity, but the entire subculture tends that way, as do most subcultures (including, in its own way, the secular, intellectual one). It is easy to see why the reflective Christian often leads a precarious existence in any subculture, particularly the conservative Christian one. In environments tainted with authoritarianism, every question creates a mini-crisis. It raises, even if only momentarily, the possibility that the belief system is flawed or incomplete. During the moment the question is in the air, before the reassuring answer can be given, unanimity teeters on the edge.

Ultimately, unanimity is impossible. It is brittle where unity is flexible and therefore strong. A single dissenter destroys it (so the dissenter may have to be dealt with harshly for the good of the group). For this reason, real questions are generally discouraged. Phony questions, however, where the answer is known by all, are part of a pleasurable ritual. They are asked and answered in a wonderful, nonthreatening confirmation of "group think." The leader voices the supposed objections of nonbelievers—the dreaded secular humanists, for example—then neatly demolishes them. The Christian movie allows twenty minutes or so of rebellion and "questioning God" on the part of its young protagonist, to be followed, as surely as day follows night, by twenty minutes of finding the way back to God and a happy ending. The audience has the thrill of the chase with none of the threat, and goes away satisfied.

The reflective Christian not only wants to ask real questions, with a sense that something is at stake, he or she also wants to broaden the range of allowable evidence in this trial of what one can believe and live for. The subculture wants only to allow approved evidence from within its own experience and tradition. (The secular intellectual world is not greatly different in this regard.) Whether it is Jerry Falwell, the Ayatollah Khomeni, or Phil Donahue, almost everyone feels at the deepest level that what they believe is reasonable and good (or at least comfortable) and that everything else is to one degree or another alien and suspect.

A reflective Christian wonders why certain writers and artists are to be read and seen, if at all, only with a hostile, defensive, error-sniffing attitude. One influential Christian speaker says Nietzsche should be burned rather than read, and suddenly, reading Nietzsche is strangely attractive. Another warns ominously that certain theologians are neo-orthodox, and one marvels at the power of a simple prefix to make something evil out of someone else's struggle to understand God.

* * * * *

His opportunity to mend fences with Dr. Shell came sooner than he wanted. After the Dean's departure, Alex spent thirty minutes staring at the lake he could not see. He had slipped into a reverie bordering on coma when a little voice deep within came to his rescue. "Coffee," it said. "Get a cup of coffee."

Alex had learned to obey this still, small voice. It had preserved him before when all his other systems had shut down. He made his way to the coffee shop, hoping to find in caffeine what his reason was unable to supply—the key to the mystery that was his life at Redeemed.

Alex took a whole pot to an empty corner table. This was

no time for half measures. Like a Buddhist before his home altar, Alex sought in his cup and saucer release from this world of struggle and pain.

It was not to be. The clouds in his brain had just begun to dissipate when a voice broke through. "Feel like sharing that pot of coffee?"

Alex didn't have to look up to know who it was. Dr. Shell's voice had always been his greatest asset. In the pulpit it could thunder or it could plead; in the classroom it bespoke author-ity—paternal, unbreachable; in the office it was calming, per-sonal. Resonant, full, pleasing, it was at all times, in all situations, a voice to be listened to.

"Sure. Have a seat. Always good to have someone to drink with."

Not, heaven knows, the right way to have put it. Alex la-mented the tightness of his own thin voice.

Dr. Shell was in his late fifties. He had a full head of wavy white hair combed straight back. A small topknot of white peaked just above his forehead. About twenty-five minutes into a really rousing sermon it would dangle down in sweaty curls in front of his eyes. His admirers had learned to look for it. Alex was conscious that his own hair was thinning prematurely.

"How's it going so far, Alex?"

"Oh, just fine. A lot of work, but I enjoy it."

"This is your first year of teaching, is it?"

"First full-time job, yes."

"Yes, I thought this was your first year."

Alex felt that coffee wasn't going to be enough.

"You know, I can still remember my first teaching job even after all these many, many years of service. I was just out of the army after World War II, and . . . By the way, Alex, did you fight over in Vietnam?"

"Ah, no. I had a medical deferment."

"Oh, I see. Anyway, I had just finished defending my coun-try when I felt the Lord calling me to go into the ministry. So I went to seminary and started teaching high school the same year. Yes, sir, those were interesting days. I can remember how cocky I was in that first teaching job. I thought I had everything figured out. I'd graduated from college before the war, had helped save the world from the Nazi scourge, and was learning Greek in seminary. What more could one need? Yes, sir, I was really full of opinions back then and ready to let everybody know them, especially my elders."

Alex was sure that Shell, in his own mind, added "and my betters."

"Yes, Alex, that first year of teaching can really be a learning experience—if one is ready to learn."

Alex had the feeling the ball was in his court now, but he wasn't sure exactly how the game was played. He decided to call a timeout.

"What subject did you teach in high school while you were going to seminary."

"English. They figured anybody could teach it back then. It is, after all, the language we all speak, isn't it? Of course, I'm sure things have changed a lot. You English teachers these days read all kinds of things I never would touch with a ten-foot pole. Actually, once I started studying the Holy Scriptures in a serious way it was hard for me to get interested in reading any other book—unless it was a book about the Bible. The Bible sort of spoils you that way, you know. Makes all those others look pretty worthless."

This was going too far. Alex decided he couldn't just take all this implicit abuse without some sort of retaliation.

"You think so?"

It came out as a question instead of a challenge.

"No, I'm exaggerating. But I thought so at one time. Actually, I've been doing a lot of nonbiblical reading the last few years. I've been trying to keep up on the humanist conspiracy."

"The what?"

"The humanist conspiracy. You know, the humanist attempt to take over our nation by destroying Christian values. Don't tell me you don't know anything about that. Anyone who's an expert on existentialism like yourself knows about humanism."

Red alert!

"Oh, humanism. Now I see what you're saying—humanism. Yes, well . . . How exactly do you define humanism?"

This was a clever (read "desperate") ploy. The old philosophical tarbaby—make them define terms until the cows come home. Every definition calls for a further definition. Each definition itself can be analyzed, quibbled with, reconsidered. Each is a punch into the tarbaby. After three or four the puncher is hopelessly entangled—a black, sticky mess. No progress made, but no ground lost either. Among hard-core academics everyone was satisfied.

Dr. Shell, alas, was no academic, hard-core or otherwise. Why punch the tarbaby when you can blow him away?

"Humanism. Are you telling me you need a definition of humanism? Why, it's everything that's been ruining this country since FDR. It's communism, liberalism, unionism, big governmentism; it's the new morality (which any fool can tell you is just the old immorality); it's homosexuals teaching our children, feminists destroying our families, evolutionists making monkeys out of us all; it's gun control, abortion on demand, handouts to every bum too lazy to work. Need I go on?"

He went on.

"Humanism is everywhere. It's in the air. It's all around. It's criminals getting five years of 'rehabilitation' for murder, it's psychiatrists who make a fortune assuring people they are not sinners, it's going off the gold standard and making our money worthless, it's TV dinners and atheism in high places."

At this point the white topknot fell into curls in front of Dr. Shell's eyes. Alex assessed the situation. He wanted to press Shell about TV dinners but was afraid his answer might sound sensible. One can only deal with so much at a time.

Actually, there was no promising response to such an outpouring. Certainly not the one Alex chose.

"That's quite a list."

"It's the condensed version, believe me. Listen, Alex, if you want to educate yourself a little, come hear Slayer next week. There's a man who's been anointed to preach the bad news of what has become of our country."

"I guess I'm having a little trouble seeing the common denominator in all those things. You sort of lost me somewhere near the beginning."

Alex clearly lacked the synthesizing powers of a conspiracy buff.

"The common denominator is crystal clear, for those with eyes to see—godlessness! Making man the measure of all things. Founding morality on whims and fickle desires. Denying the relevance of anything transcendent to human endeavors."

Where did one begin? Start with one of his truths and affirm common ground? With one of his half-truths and try the "yes, but . . ." technique? Or with one of his outrageous falsehoods to clear away the garbage? Alex made his choice quickly.

"More coffee?"

"No thanks. I've got a class—Introduction to Philosophy in three minutes."

"That's how long it takes you to introduce them to philosophy?"

"No, that's when the class begins, Adamson. The accrediting board thought we should have a philosophy course here so the President said okay, at least until we get accreditation. He insisted that I teach it, however."

Dr. Shell got up to leave. Alex's appetite for self-abuse got the better of him.

"What are you studying in there these days?"

"Romans. Helps them learn to think logically."

*   *   *   *   *

Enemies of the church would like to paint it as cynical and Machiavellian in its use of power. What is easier than caricaturing the church (as so often happens in popular culture) as hypocritical, intolerant, blue-nosed naysayers who delight in squashing youth, loveliness, freedom, and intelligence? Except in the most extreme cases, it simply isn't so. This is as phony a boogeyman as any created by the church itself regarding the larger culture. Like those, however, it has just enough basis in truth to make it powerful and persistent.

Unfortunately, too many wounded Christians also indulge in this condescending attitude. There is a sarcastic bite to their use of the phrase "the church" that suggests they bear no responsibility for its failings. Whether through their exposure to secular critics of religion, their greater intelligence, or their broader experience, they have, thankfully, been liberated from the pathetic narrowness which still afflicts others. Adapting the superior attitude they elsewhere condemn, they, like the Pharisee in Christ's parable (Luke 18:11), thank God that they are not like other Christians: narrow, legalistic, unsophisticated.

Narrowness, hypocrisy, intolerance aplenty have always been in the church, which is to say the church has always been made up of human beings. But there has always been the Spirit of God, also, moving to work His will in His ways, human failure notwithstanding. One manifestation of that spirit, missing from the standard caricature of the church, is the genuine concern it often feels for the struggling Christian, even if that concern is sometimes shown in heavy-handed ways.

The church often feels like the rescuer trying to talk the would-be suicide victim off the ledge. Nothing could be clearer to the rescuer than that jumping, no matter what the reasons, would be a disastrously wrong decision. Talk about respecting the person's right to choose, or the possibility that he might survive the jump after all, strikes the rescuer as irrelevant, irresponsible, even criminal. The church, in short, often cares about the ultimate fate of the dissenter in a way no one else ever will. Those who would "free" him or her from religious illusion seemingly have very little to offer in place of faith, being not much different from those in the street who shout for the person to jump.

The reflective Christian's relationship to the church, then, is varied and complex. Much of the difficulty that arises stems from an inadequate awareness on both sides of the dual nature of the church as an instrument of God's work and, at the same time, a culturally bound monument to human fallenness.

Many accede to the church's identification of its ways with God's ways. They are presented with an entire package labeled "the Christian faith," which is actually composed of many extra elements—the idiosyncratic traditions of that specific branch of Christendom, particular political and social views, a set of attitudes toward the larger culture, personal preferences and prejudices, and so on.

The Christian in this situation too often adopts the false either-or thinking of the subculture. Some keep their questions and concerns concealed, as likely to condemn themselves for lack of faith as to question whether the concept of faith they have been presented is adequate. Like rape victims who suffer the added trauma of being badgered by a defense lawyer at a trial, many wounded Christians have learned that revealing their thoughts compounds their difficulties, especially in the conservative church.

Others, as they find themselves in ever greater tension with their environment, feel they must either silence a fundamental part of themselves and conform to expectations, or reject the entire package they have been offered and make do without God. They have internalized the often inaccurate equation of their church and subculture with God and His work, and in rejecting one, they mistakenly reject the other.

These people need to understand what Kierkegaard understood so well: not only is Christendom not synonymous with a life in Christ, following Christ may well require rejecting parts of Christendom. The church is continually tempted to confuse its mission to spread and embody the "good news" with the need every organization feels to perpetuate and enhance itself. Karl Barth identified the difference when he said, "Ministration of the word is not *ad* ministration, however smoothly it may go." [3] The reflective Christian should be sensitive to the difference as well, affirming and committing himself or herself to those parts of a Christian subculture which honestly attempt to do God's work, while staying free, as much as possible, from the inevitable distortions that abound wherever human beings are found.

This is not an easy task. The potential for self-deception and false solutions is great. Leaving the church entirely is rarely the answer. Tragically, the illusions and misconceptions of the Christian subculture often drive the wounded into illusions and misconceptions of a different kind. They substitute one inadequate conception of the world for another, losing in the process that core relationship to God which redeems all our errors.

Preserving and strengthening that relationship to God and living out its implications in an undiscerning and troubled world is the great challenge to the Christian. For all its failings, the church as a whole is an ally in that cause. The reflective Christian can draw great strength and insight from it if he sees clearly what it is and is not, forgiving the church its trespasses as he is forgiven his own.

3

The Reflective Christian in the Secular World of Ideas

Discovering the Church is apt to be a slow procedure but it can only take place if you have a free mind and no vested interest in disbelief....
—Flannery O'Connor

No one is so terribly deceived as he who does not himself suspect it....
—Kierkegaard

Happy is the man who is not scandalized by me.
—Jesus Christ

IN THEORY THE REFLECTIVE CHRISTIAN should be at home in the secular world of ideas, and in practice many are. Nothing in the essential nature of either Christianity or intellectual and creative endeavor is inherently contradictory, as many centuries of Christian leadership in forming culture have shown. Because of education, career, or simple inclination, reflective Christians often participate in this world of the making, propagating, and defending of ideas and images.

This is how it should be. Christians should be getting dirt under their fingernails in almost every area of interest to human beings. The common distinction between the sacred and the secular, while occasionally valid, often obscures the greater reality that God made the WHOLE world and is not willing that any of it be the sole province of those who have turned from Him.

Conservative Christians have too long been paranoid about the world just beyond our noses. Much of the defensiveness and anger that we direct toward the "secularists" spring more from insecurity and fear than from informed righteousness. The so-called secular world is sometimes not nearly so much a threat to God and His ways, as it is to us and our ways.

This admonition against Christian paranoia should be balanced, however, with an insistence on Christian realism. The secular world *does*, by and large, ignore God (though they often unknowingly affirm His truths), and such ignorance has decisive consequences. The better I understand the character of this world, the less I will fall prey to its illusions and the more I can contribute within it.

Having defended participation in this world, I nonetheless have a question for myself. Why, as a college teacher, do I dislike going to professional conferences? My reasons aren't all rational. Part of it may come from my first big convention years ago in Chicago where I fruitlessly searched for a job while a fellow in the elevator expressed weariness at having to decide whether to take the offer from Harvard or the one from Johns Hopkins or one of the four others he had received. Envy is an ugly thing.

Much of it is the great amount of posturing and puffery that goes on. Academics display their tail feathers to each other like peacocks in the barnyard. Thirty minutes of intense name-dropping is more tiring than running a marathon, and not as interesting.

But, truthfully, I am uncomfortable at such gatherings at least in part because I feel like an alien. I am not one of them. I do not want to be one of them. We share the same discipline, the same love of literature, similar classroom experiences, and so on. But at the deepest level, we literally do not live in the same world. My values are not their values, my truths are not their truths, my sense of why I am here on this earth is far from theirs.

Is this paranoia? Is this narrowness? Is this a simple failure to appreciate diversity? I hope not. Because I do learn from these people. Some of them I greatly respect and even admire. Many I personally like. I do not desire to be surrounded with clones of myself that parrot back to me my own beliefs.

And it is not that this is all I think about in such situations. On the contrary, it is more often a preconscious feeling to which I only occasionally pay attention. I listen to speakers and engage in professional banter like everyone else.

I cannot clearly articulate what I feel even to myself. Perhaps it is that there is little hope of making myself known to these people. The language of my innermost being is gibberish to their ears—literally nonsense. I see things where they are sure that nothing exists to be seen. I hear things where for them is only empty silence.

I do not think my discomfort is a fear of rejection so much as an awareness that I will be responded to as something other than what I am. If I maintain my role as an academic, or a good old boy, there is no problem. But to the extent that I reveal what makes me tick, what shapes my whole view of reality, I am not likely, in the brief exchanges to which one is limited in these settings, to be much more than a caricature, an anachronism, an object of condescension or a raised eyebrow and a knowing look.

I realize full well that this overstates the case. There are others in such gatherings who are believers as well, and still more who are very accepting of belief. I am not speaking at all of that favorite Christian cliché of being persecuted for witnessing to my faith, but of that subtle sense of alienation that comes when one is "other," when one does not quite fit, when, in Martin Buber's terms, one is an "it" and not a "thou." And likely this is how the secularist feels in a Christian setting, because I have sometimes felt this way in Christian circles myself.

There are, of course, many different responses to religious belief in the secular world of ideas. They range from tolerance to indifference to condescension to open hostility. For many, religious belief is so irrelevant to their interests and conceptions that they cannot imagine it playing a central role in any serious matter or in any intelligent person's life. They illustrate T. S. Eliot's observation that secularism in our century is not simply disbelief in the supernatural but a total inability even to conceive of transcendence.[1]

To others, religion is out-dated at best and, at worst, an age-old instrument of oppression. It is a roadblock to knowledge and freedom that must finally be eliminated in our march to enlightenment. If to be considered at all, it is as a historical phenomenon, one among a multitude, that can be analyzed, categorized, and filed in our endless cataloging of the various activities of humankind.

Personal religious faith threatens one of the sacred tenets of contemporary intellectual orthodoxy: doubt everything. To the secularist, Christian intellectuals are touchingly naive, refusing to submit one area of their lives (that of faith) to the same high standards of analysis and evidence that they, as intellectuals, apply in all others. Faith supposedly cannot survive such scrutiny, and holding to it therefore betrays either weakness or dishonesty.

Religious faith itself, however, does not usually get you in trouble in this subculture so much as allowing that faith out of its box so that it pokes its nose where it does not belong. Many are perfectly content to allow a fellow intellectual to practice a private faith. After all, some people are into jogging or stereo equipment, and others are "into" God. The trouble begins when it appears that your faith has influenced (contaminated) your thinking in other areas. Worse yet is to imply that your religious outlook has given you insights to which the secularist is blind.

There is a great irony in the relationship of the reflective Christian to the two subcultures I am discussing. You can get in hot water in the Christian world precisely for being too insistently Christian. Nothing is as irritating to legalistic fundamentalists (not all are) as the suggestion that their behavior is not up to biblical standards.

Likewise, the reflective Christian is often at odds with the secularist intellectual for being truly reflective, for applying the intellectual's tools of analysis, reason, and doubt against the secularist's own presuppositions. Reflecting critically on secularist orthodoxy will draw just as much fire in this world, which supposedly prizes reflection, as questioning religious orthodoxy will in the other.

Secularists don't generally think of themselves as having an orthodoxy, but they have one just the same. It is composed of various articles of faith, each with its own history. These articles of secular orthodoxy revolve around concepts like reason, inquiry, objectivity, tolerance, evidence, individualism, creativity, truth, justice, and so on. My aim is not to attack this intellectual faith; it is powerful, often beneficial, and not inherently incompatible with religious faith (in which many of these values originated). But the reflective Christian in this subculture should understand how tenuous and elusive these concepts often are in practice. The level of hypocrisy here is very high, and one should give only as much credibility to the secularists as they are due, not as much as they claim.

One of the myths of secular orthodoxy to which I have already alluded is that the secular, intellectual community relies primarily on reasoned analysis of evidence while religious faith is mere wishing or an uncritical clinging to tradition. The secularist often appeals to reason as though it were some transcendent, immutable faculty to which all thinking people have access and which can be employed at will to separate truth from error.

This common view fails to distinguish between logic—which is a tightly defined, highly controlled use of precise rules of reasoning and which has an important but limited area of application in the human experience—and the whole mental process of generating beliefs, opinions, points of view, and daily explanations of our experience in the world. The latter is what is going on 95 percent of the time when people, including intellectuals, use words like *reason,* or *thinking,* and it is far from a pure and predictable process.

Rather than a food processor which slices, dices, and purees reality at the operator's command, giving everyone who uses it correctly similar results, reason in this second sense is more like Saturday's soup made out of the week's leftovers. It is the nice neat name we give to a mishmash of interrelated forces which includes personality traits and idiosyncrasies, prejudice, emotions, intellectual fads, felt needs, cultural conditioning, and, at times, indigestion. The soup never tastes the same twice in a row. To imply that this process arrives at something greatly more certain and trustworthy than religious faith is simply naive.

Related to this is the myth of objectivity. Objectivity supposedly flows from the unbiased use of this universal instrument called reason. Just as two people can use the same scale to measure different things, thereby relating them to an objective standard, so, theoretically, can one use this thing called reason to objectively evaluate evidence and generate insight into the nature of reality. Objectivity is supposedly something the intellectual can have, while the person of faith wallows in mere subjectivity.

In the narrow application of logic to limited problems, some degree of objectivity is perhaps possible. But in the broil of the wider human enterprise, in deciding what is good and true and beautiful and worth living for in this world, there is so much sheer humanness at work (and there should be), that the claim of cool, rational objectivity is almost laughable. Only objects are truly objective.

I am not arguing that reason is useless, only that the secular world cannot rightfully claim superiority or intimidate the person of faith based on its use. The Christian not only can use reason as well as the secularist, he or she is more likely to be properly aware of its limitations. The precarious and limited nature of reason is an insight provided by reason itself (and by many secular thinkers over the last 150 years). My reservations about reason are commonplace in some parts of the secular world, but much of the rest of secularism acts as though it has the ultimate weapon in the battle for truth which the person of faith, by definition, has forfeited.

* * * * *

The weekend would last no longer than all weekends, the location of the conference was only eighty-five miles away, but the distance between it and Alex's life at Redeemed could only be measured in light years. All that frustrated, confounded, and diminished him at Redeemed would be left behind for a few days while, among people who valued the mind, he renewed his ties to the life of free inquiry, the love of reflection, and the pursuit of truth.

"Bull. That's all we're going to hear from Lebarge tonight—bull. His last book was filled with it. Of course it won the Dunkirk Prize, but then what do you expect? Did you see who was on the Dunkirk selection committee?"

He didn't wait for Alex to respond, which was just as well. Alex didn't have the slightest idea who was on the Dunkirk committee. It didn't help that he had also never heard of the Dunkirk Prize. Or the book for which it was awarded. Or, to be depressingly honest, tonight's keynote speaker.

"Lionel Hughes! Can you believe it? Lionel Hughes directed

Lebarge's dissertation on semiotics twenty years ago, and then he turns out to be the head of the Dunkirk selection committee that gives Lebarge the prize for his book on Derrida. That's rich. Can you believe it?"

Alex smiled faintly as he nodded that he could, in fact, believe it, just as soon as he worked up enough interest to care. What did interest him right now was how to get away from this fellow. He had made the mistake of asking him the time of the evening keynote address. All this extra information came at no additional charge.

"Where are you from, anyway, uh . . . let's see, what does your name tag say. . . ?"

"Alex."

"Alex. You from the university here, Alex?"

"No. No. Not hardly. I teach at, uh, a small college north of here. No place you'd ever have heard of."

"Well, let me tell you, be glad you're teaching at a small college. I'm at UNK and it's a real snake pit. You can't believe the games those cretins play there. I've got a book and six articles published in five years and they're hassling my rear about whether I'm going to get tenure or not. Fact is, they don't want to give it to me because they have no tenured women in the department and they're worried about a sex bias suit. Hell, if I don't get tenure I'll slap a reverse discrimination suit on them so fast they won't be able to tell dactyls from ducktails."

His manufactured anger dissolved as he contemplated the cleverness of his word play.

"Say, Alex. You don't have a drink in your hand. How do you expect to make it through one of these ghastly conferences without steady libations? A man shouldn't have to listen to Lebarge sober. That's cruel and unusual punishment, don't you think?"

"Not right now, thanks. I've got to go back to my room for a minute. It's been nice talking to you."

"Right. Let me give you a tip. After the bull session tonight with Lebarge, UC is having an open bar in the Coconut Room.

It's supposed to be for their staff and alumni only, but heaven knows they won't be checking."

"Okay. Thanks for the tip. Maybe I'll see you there."

Strangely enough, the man was right about the keynote address. An impressive pastiche of insider anecdotes, sly comments, arcane observations, and deft manipulation of jargon—the obvious was obfuscated, the mysteries invoked, all simmered in condescension and deflation, served warm to an appreciative audience of ravenous gourmets.

Afterward, Alex inquired about the location of the Coconut Room, and headed in the opposite direction.

* * * * *

Perhaps the most fundamental tenet of current secular orthodoxy is also the most frequently violated. If there is any quality with which the wide world of ideas proudly contrasts itself with conservative Christianity, it is tolerance—specifically tolerance of difference and diversity. Secular intellectuals, so the myth goes, are willing to let people be different, are interested in allowing all points of view to exist simultaneously, while religious types are narrow, exclusive, and insist on their own way. If there were Ten Commandments of Secular Orthodoxy, "Thou shall be tolerant of all points of view" would certainly be one of them.

Unfortunately, the hypocrisy in this regard is staggering. As I mentioned in discussing the psychology of belief, the secular world is generally only tolerant of the kind of diversity already approved by its framework. Acceptable diversity might include different views on how the world's wealth should be distributed, on whether capital punishment is just, on the relative merits of particular writers or artists, even on whether God exists or not. What is not to be tolerated, currently, are any views that make absolute claims, particularly if they suggest that all competing views are in error. Not only will such a claim be dismissed as a medieval anachronism, especially in nonscientific fields, it will often be dismissed simply because it is an absolute claim, not on any serious consideration of the merits of the claim itself.

The orthodoxy of the day, then, is pluralism—the free (and inconclusive) play of multitudinous perspectives. Any questioning of this orthodoxy is heresy, punishable by ostracism, ridicule, neglect, or whatever other means necessary. Ironically, most pluralists don't really believe in pluralism. True difference, something which questions the basic validity of the secular, intellectual enterprise, is a threat to the existence of the subculture and not to be tolerated. Only "friendly" diversity, like the pseudo-questions in the Christian subculture, can be allowed. The intellectual world, like its Christian counterpart, exercises power first for the purpose of self-preservation, and only much less for the sake of intangible qualities such as truth.

I do not want in this slightly caricatured sketch of the secular world of ideas to encourage the long-standing phobia in fundamentalist Christian circles regarding things intellectual and artistic. The failures and foolishness in this part of the human endeavor are no more reason for the Christian to withdraw from it than like shortcomings are adequate reason to abandon the church.

The Christian who is inclined and equipped should make the greatest contribution possible to the wide range of human activities. We should be the first to do many good things, not the ones dragged reluctantly into the modern world. We also should expect to learn much of value from nonbelievers in the process. They too, it is rumored, are made in the image of God.

But we must also recognize that this subculture is generally unsympathetic to the central convictions and commitments of a person of faith. The believer feels pressure, internal as much as external, to be defensive regarding his or her world view, to hold it almost apologetically, as though it were embarrassingly old-fashioned and self-indulgent in the midst of high-powered, confident competitors.

In truth, the secular world is greatly confused and fragmented. For all its accomplishments in specialized areas, it has largely abandoned any pretense of providing a coherent account of life. Its effort to make a virtue out of this failing by deifying pluralism and relativism is a measure of its desperation. The person bringing religious insights to such a sorry state of affairs has no reason to apologize or feel defensive.

Even this brief discussion suggests how much these two subcultures have in common, and why a reflective Christian might have trouble in both. Each creates an orthodoxy of belief and behavior, and rewards or punishes based on adherence to written and unwritten standards. Doubtless this is true for all subcultures, but the similarities are startling in two groups which claim to be so different from each other.

Neither subculture, for instance, will seriously consider arguments or evidence which threatens its orthodoxy. One expects this, perhaps, with religious institutions, but they are not alone. A local public university of national stature conducted a conference on the threat of creationism to public science education and did not invite any creationists to speak. Another university asked an extension course teacher to take his class on "marriage and the family" off campus because his reading material offended the liberal bias of the university community. The examples are endless on both sides.

Each of these groups tends to reject the other with little if any understanding of what they are rejecting. I have sat through sermons denouncing "secular humanism" that would have been hilarious in their ignorance and paranoia had they not been so tragically influential on their rapt audiences. Likewise, I am frequently amazed at the shallow and distorted conceptions many intelligent and educated people have regarding the Christian faith. One can only wonder, for instance, that a man so reputedly brilliant as Bertrand Russell could have so little insight into what he was rejecting in his famous essay, "Why I Am Not a Christian."

The end product of ignorance plus confidence is smugness, and both subcultures are bountifully supplied. Each feels it holds the high ground—the Christians morally, the secularists

both morally and intellectually. The legendary self-righteousness of Christians has nothing on an offended intellectual in
full-blown indignation. The clichés of belief and disbelief are
equally maddening. One doesn't escape clichés by leaving the
Christian subculture; one merely trades formulaic expressions
of an essential truth for clichés which express something less.

*   *   *   *   *

As he headed away from the Coconut Room, Alex felt an
unnameable irritation. He had witnessed a moment set aside
for the celebration of language reduced to a self-aggrandizing
display, but was only conscious of feeling mildly depressed.

Intimate troikas sporting pipes and elbow patches filled the
lobby with earnest conversation and smoke. Great things, it
seemed, were being done.

Alex decided to return to his room to read the free copy
of King Kenner's latest book which he had scrounged at the
bookstalls. As he moved in the direction of the elevator, someone fired his name from close range.

"Adamson!"

Alex turned with a certain hopefulness that proved greatly
premature. It was Garrison Adler, an acquaintance from graduate school days whose dissertation on a Freudian interpretation of the imagery of Alexander Pope was, last he'd heard,
going into its third year of writing with no sign that the gold
mine was about to give out.

"Hello, Garrison. It's been a long time."

"I should say it has! Good to see you. Let me introduce
you to my friend here. Deidre, this is Alex Adamson. Alex,
this is Deidre Everett."

Deidre nodded with an energy-conserving smile.

"Well, what are you doing these days, Adamson? Teaching
somewhere?"

"Well, in a way. A small college north of here. You wouldn't
have heard of it."

"Oh don't be so sure. I sent out two hundred dossiers when
I passed my orals, some to places so small they only hold

graduation ceremonies on leap years. What's the name of it?"

"Well, it's called Redeemed College."

Deidre snorted. "Redeemed College. Must have been started by either a trading stamp magnate or a TV preacher."

"Yes, it is a church-related school. Not exactly what I had in mind when I broke my back getting a Ph.D., but then I guess a lot of people in our program never ended up teaching at all."

"Like me, for example," Garrison interjected. "You know Adamson, I never did finish my dissertation—even though I think Oxford would have published it. Jill got sick of supporting me and made me go to work. I've been working for Bache this last year as an investment counselor. At first I kicked myself for selling out. Can you believe a hard-core humanities-type like me ending up in the quid pro quo world of big securities?"

"Does seem a bit strange Garrison. Weren't you the local champion of Marxist criticism for a few years?"

"Yah, that was me. You know how to hurt a guy Adamson. But you know what I discovered? I found out that managing a portfolio was like writing a poem. There's a rhythm to it, a certain sense of elegance and proportion. You have to analyze and synthesize while maintaining an intuitive sense of the whole. And if everything is put together just right, with a mixture of sweat and inspiration, you have a creation you can take some pride in."

"And a few trips to Hawaii on," added Deidre with the faint air of a put-down.

Alex decided against pursuing Garrison's literary theory of investments in favor of a safer question.

"What brings you to a convention like this then?"

"Oh, I'm only here because Deidre's leading one of the sessions. You probably didn't hear that Jill and I split a few months ago. Once I was working at Bache we found we didn't have much in common. It was a tough time. I wouldn't have made it through if it hadn't been for Deidre. She's my rock. We've been together since the breakup."

And that was the safe question, Alex thought to himself.

As he searched for an exit line, Garrison changed the subject.

"You should go to the session Deidre's chairing tomorrow. It's titled 'Education and the Menace of the New Right.'"

"That should be interesting," Alex said as unironically as possible, turning his gaze to Deidre. "What exactly are you going to deal with?"

Deidre took a deep breath like she was laying up stock for a major offensive. Alex cast around in his mind for the nearest foxhole.

"I'll tell Alex all about it, Garrison, if you'll go and get us something to drink. It's hotter than hades in here!"

"I'm off. Be sure to tell him about the *Catcher in the Rye* petition."

"Oh my, the petition. Whatever you get, make mine a double."

"Right, what for you Alex?"

"Oh, nothing for me, thanks."

Garrison departed, seemingly pleased to have an important mission laid to his charge.

"Don't tell me you don't drink, Alex. I've never met any of Garrison's grad school cronies whose level of interest didn't depend on the amount of booze in their brains at any given time."

"Well I do and I don't. Uh, that is, I never did much and now I don't at all. It's sort of complicated."

"Complicated?"

"Well, actually, the school I teach at doesn't allow me to drink; . . . ah, rather I should say, I've committed myself not to drink."

Alex had not witnessed such stunned disbelief since Joe Namath's Jets beat Baltimore in Superbowl III.

"You have got to be kidding!" Deidre said each word slowly, with heartfelt emphasis. "You simply have got to be kidding!" Alex considered for an instant the possible advantages of pretending that he had been. Deidre didn't wait.

"Holy mother of God. This is the twentieth century last I checked. Are people still getting away with this kind of thing?

Why it's fascism. It's——fascism. This is the most depressing thing I've heard this week. How can you let yourself participate in something like that?"

Where to start? One might as well try to explain to a grand dragon of the Klu Klux Klan that Christ was a Jew.

"Well, I wouldn't call it fascism. I . . ."

"What would you call it?"

"Well, you need to understand some of the history of these people. They . . ."

"I am sure the history of mass illusion, intolerance, and totalitarianism has its charms, but I don't think I'd be ready for it without a few rounds of Scotch first."

"It really isn't as bad as it sounds. You see, these people believed they should be sort of set apart in some ways from society as a whole, and . . ."

"They're set apart all right. So are monkeys in a cage. Listen, Alex, if these people don't want to drink that's fine. Maybe we should all drink less. But when they go telling other normal people, which I'm assuming you are, that they can't drink either, that's fascism. And if you go along with it, then you're aiding and abetting fascism. I'm not being judgmental, mind you, because that's fascist, too, but all of us have got to do what we can to stop these New Right stormtroopers from destroying this country. It may be just prohibitions against drinking now, but you only have to open your eyes to see that this country is going to hell in a handcart! They want to control who we have sex with, how big our families are, what we read, what we watch, what we teach our kids. Next, they'll be telling me I have to shave my legs!"

There was no good exit line for this conversation. Alex decided to do without one. Self-preservation came before decorum.

"That's a very interesting point, Ms. Everett." He emphasized the *z* sound and threw up a weak smoke screen for a precipitous retreat. "I'll try to make your workshop tomorrow, but I've got to be running along now."

"But I haven't told you about the petition."

"Maybe after the workshop. Give my regrets to Garrison. It's been nice talking with you."

Alex smiled apologetically as he backed into the haze. He turned, fixing his eyes on the elevator doors across the lobby. For him they were the technological equivalent of Dante's spiraling path up Mount Purgatory—somewhere up above was the paradisiacal calm of his hotel room.

As the door opened one final obstacle presented itself. Off stepped the fellow he had met earlier who had told him all one could ever want to know about the Dunkirk Award.

"Say, it's you again. You won't believe this. The jerks from UNK wouldn't let me into their open bar party in the Coconut Room. Can you believe that?"

This time Alex felt he could. Wordlessly, he jumped into the empty elevator just as the doors quietly closed.

*   *   *   *   *

Where can I stand in all this? Each subculture welcomes me if I swear allegiance to the ruling orthodoxy of thought and behavior. And I am a compliant enough fellow to embrace orthodoxy if I think it is true. In fact, I am greatly attracted to *both* orthodoxies. I feel both the claims of faith, for I have tasted transcendence, and the logic of pluralism, for does not my own mind itself generate many ways of seeing and thinking?

But each group is impatient with the recalcitrant who wants to retain parts of both worlds. Conservative Christendom will allow you to think, as long as you think "correctly," or keep dangerous thoughts to yourself. The secular world will allow you to be a Christian, as long as your faith is kept in quarantine and not allowed to influence your judgments or lead you to question secular presuppositions.

Like everyone, reflective Christians want to be accepted, to be valued, to be liked—ultimately to be secure. We are afraid of looking stupid, especially if we have an intellectual bent, but even more afraid, I hope, of *being* stupid. That is, I am willing, reluctantly, to be out of sync in either or both subcultures—to appear alternately naive or rebellious, outdated or backslidden—if I am convinced that my stand is the right one.

Ah, there's the rub. Will reflection ever give one peace about "the right" position? Intellectual orthodoxy will allow at best "*a* right" position, though even that is suspect. "How," the ever-inquiring mind asks, "can I know that what I believe is right? Contrary forces witness to conflicting truths. I think I have the courage to take a stand, if only I could be sure where that stand should be."

Both subcultures are eager to help—one by offering a culture-soaked religious institution, the other by encouraging us to accept, even celebrate, the supermarket of ideas and the privatization of values. I desire the approval of both, but not by segregating or destroying an essential part of myself. I find truth and distortion in each. My own temperament, mind, and experiences unfit me for whole-hearted, unthinking embracing of either, but also make impossible total abandonment of either. I have been touched by God, yet suspect that not everything in the church is of God. Attracted to the beauty, power, and understanding available in the secular world of ideas, I see at the same time the inevitable illusions that arise from ignoring the source of all beauty, power, and insight.

Common sense solutions are often not solutions at all. Why not identify, for instance, with the liberal church which seems more free of authoritarianism, legalism, and anti-world paranoia? Wouldn't this be the best of both worlds? More likely the worst of both worlds, I'm afraid.

The liberal church solves the problems of the reflective believer by allowing the secular world to determine what issues are important and in what terms those issues will be addressed. Its utmost priority is to be up-to-date and relevant. By taking its definition of relevance from secular society rather than from the God against whom the significance of all things is measured, it risks making itself instead one of the most irrelevant institutions on earth. (This is a harsh judgment. I am willing to be convinced otherwise by those who have more experience in that part of Christendom than I do.)

If both the conservative and liberal church have such problems, why not simply leave the church altogether while retaining an individual faith in God? Conceivable, but rarely beneficial in the long run. The weakness of the church is merely the weakness on a corporate scale of individual human beings. Leave the church and you take many of its weaknesses with you, leaving behind its greatest and compensating strengths.

This, in my experience, is the dilemma of many reflective Christians. They are caught between two worlds (these are only two of many). Both make claims too strong to be ignored. The smug self-righteousness of neither is justified. God's will and work is not coterminous with the conservative Christian world as it claims. Neither is reason, learning, humaneness, and insight the sole possession of secular thought.

Many have not articulated this dilemma clearly for themselves. They feel pressures, internal and external, which they often do not consciously recognize and whose source they do not identify. They frequently are wounded without knowing it, and their wounds take many forms. A student remarks to me, "I have decided to keep believing in God, but I could never tell anyone else they should." Is this praiseworthy recognition of the private nature of belief or paralysis from an uncritical acceptance of pluralist propaganda?

Another talented and intelligent young woman responds to the extreme legalism of her preacher's-daughter upbringing by consciously violating as many of its prohibitions as possible. Is this a healthy liberation from a narrow ideology or the substitution of the folly of license for the folly of legalism?

The son of a Christian college professor finds the theology and world view of his upbringing inadequate and not respected in the larger world of ideas to which he is attracted. In his eagerness to please new friends whose approval now means so much, he jettisons any aspects of his faith which they find offensive.

One reflective Christian fears that thinking too much will only lead him away from God. Having suppressed his questions in the name of faith, all seems well, but a part of him is dead. Another feels keenly the suffering and injustice in the world. Seeing the church's hypocrisy and its eagerness to protect the status quo convinces her that Christianity has nothing to offer, and she abandons (or is abandoned by?) the faith of her youth.

The examples seem endless even in my own limited experience. The afflicted include pastors, professors, professionals, and laborers, as well as young people putting together their own world view for the first time. The problem cuts across lines of education, gender, class, and age, and it includes both many who are just inside the circle of faith and many who are just outside.

I would not claim that this is "the great problem facing the church today," only that some people lead diminished lives because of it. I also am not offering "ten steps" or "the key" to solving the problem and leading a "dynamic Christian life." I am enough of a twentieth-century man to be suspicious of such talk and to believe that there are a great variety of God-honoring ways to respond to the dilemmas of faith and life. What I do offer are simply some reflections of my own and a small part of my personal response to the situation I have described, in the hope that some will find them helpful.

4

The Search for Truth and Certainty

Seeing too much to deny and too little to be sure, I am in a state to be pitied.
—Pascal

It would seem very strange that Christianity should have come into the world just to receive an explanation....
—Kierkegaard

TRUTH, REASON, FAITH—what a knotty complex of forces. Consider *truth*. I have an almost physical reaction to the word. It sets off a whole string of positive associations in my mind and emotions: goodness, beauty, justice, love, the Dodgers (late Brooklyn, early Los Angeles). Who does not want truth, even if they don't give it a moment's thought? Even the foolish man who asked a friend of mine recently, "When are you going to admit there's nothing as important in life as making a hell of a lot of money?" hopes desperately this is the truth, lest he discover that he has wasted the only life he will get.

How to find truth, that is the question, and how to know that one has found it. Nothing has so occupied reflective men and women for as long as we have record; nothing has elicited more anguish and struggle. Nothing, also, has created such a climate for despair and irresponsibility as the modern conviction that the word no longer has much meaning.

Of the many possible avenues to truth, two of the most traveled are *reason* and *faith*. What simple names for activities so complex and diverse by themselves, let alone when brought into relationship with one another. Many extol the virtues of reason or of faith, or of the two together, with only the slimmest understanding of what each entails.

Who would claim to explain with precision the exact nature of these things and their proper role in our lives? What is this thing we call, with touching simplicity, "thinking"? What is reason, its uses, its limits? What is the relation between thinking, reflecting, and reason? What is faith and how does it relate to reason? Might they really be two aspects of the same faculty? Is dividing our mental/spiritual life into separate "faculties" itself a distortion? Is faith reasonable, unreasonable, or nonreasonable? Does either reason or faith yield certainty? Happiness?

The questions go on forever because the reflecting process has no required stopping point. But you and I do not go on forever. At some point we feel compelled to interrupt the process and demand a decision of the reflecting mind regarding what is true, what we can affirm and build a life on. In certain cases the mind cooperates—buy this stock, join that political party, get out of the way of this charging bull. On questions of a more ultimate nature, however, like our possible relationship to God, the great filibuster of the mind is harder to break. Reflection on infinite things seems to call, almost by definition, for infinite reflection.

So we engage in this process called reason, and we exercise this thing called faith, secularists as much as anyone, and we hope to end up with something approximating what for many centuries we have called truth. And what is meant by all these terms is never quite the same, neither from person to person, nor from age to age.

So far I may sound like the typical modern relativist whose next revelation is that truth is a purely subjective projection of cultural conditioning and that we have no honest alternative to paddling around in the pluralist soup. I neither believe that nor agree that logic requires that position. My aim is modest: to consider some of the prevalent attitudes toward these concepts in our two subcultures and to suggest an outlook that is at the same time realistic and compatible with a life of faith and commitment.

The historical development of our conceptions of reason—what it is and what it can do for us—is interesting in its own right. Significantly, most of the views which have ever existed can be found operating today in some part of our culture. Two of the most common attitudes are also two of the most extreme. One part of our culture, led by science, exalts reason as the primary, if not only, human tool for understanding our existence. Another part, with numerous allies in the humanities, denigrates reason as a tyrannical faculty which is not only closed to great portions of reality, but, as the ills of our technological age prove, may be our greatest enemy.

Historically, the church has a rich tradition of a healthy use of reason. In our century, however, the conservative church has been attracted to both these unhealthy extremes. Fundamentalist Protestantism, for instance, derived its peculiar character in the early years of this century from an aggressively anti-intellectual, anti-world stance. Feeling the fundamentals of the faith threatened by secular intellectualism, it tended to consign reason, with all its dangerous byproducts (liberalism, doubt, science), to Satan's camp and to glory in a simplistic faith that finds expression in such rallying cries as, "The Bible says it! I believe it! That's good enough for me!"

A competing Christian apologetic, having both scholarly and popularized forms, has been heavily rationalistic, emphasizing such concepts as absolutes, evidences, and reasonable faith. This is largely an attempt to fight secularism with its own weapons or, it might be argued, with weapons provided by God which secularists have misused. This approach rejects the image of people of faith as naive obscurantists and is very attractive to many reflective Christians. In theory it has much to recommend it; in practice it can distort both the reality of God and the nature of our relationship with Him.

We discussed briefly in the last chapter a few misconceptions about reason that are particularly common in the secular world. Rather than something only secular intellectuals use, reason is equally used and misused by both secularists and believers. While a very powerful tool, reason is not nearly as dominant in our thinking, feeling, reflecting lives as many assume. It is only one part of a tangled complex of forces—ranging from idiosyncrasies of personality and experience to general cultural and historical conditioning—that help shape what we believe.

There is no objective, neutral thing called "reason" which anyone with some training can use to get at the "truth" of things (especially nonphysical things). The closest we come perhaps is in the scientific method of hypothesis and experimentation or in the technical use of logic in formal philosophy, but in many areas of life these approaches are not very helpful. Much more often, our "reasoning" is really that everything-including-the-kitchen-sink process discussed in the previous chapter. It is a process that can produce error as easily as truth or, even more dangerous, a subtle combination of the two. And it will not do to say that reason only yields error when used incorrectly. With the big issues of life, there is no guaranteed "correct" way for using reason. In these situations, reasoning is protean, changing shapes at will.

The reasoning process does not first serve truth, but rather the needs of the person exercising it. It is the genie in the bottle, willing to do whatever its master bids—and, like the genie, not caring particularly who the master is. Do you have a position and, more importantly, a sense of security that needs defending? Call on reason and it will generate defenses ad infinitum. Have you changed your position? Nothing to worry about, the reasoning process is infinitely adaptable.

But what of evidence? Isn't it objective, something fixed that limits the fickleness of reasoning? Not significantly. All evidence requires interpretation. Nothing "out there" is evidence until it has been brought "in here," into my argument, to be used as I see fit. In politics, religion, family relations, and every other human endeavor, opposing sides use the same evidence to defend contradictory positions.

Are the denigrators of reason right, then? No, though their insights must be carefully considered. Those who disparage reason, ironically, often use reason to do so. They offer arguments, "reasons," why reason is worthless. Reason isn't worthless at all, but my reason is operating best when it makes clear to me what it can and cannot do. As long as it does not claim too much it should not be ridiculed for its limitations any more than our physical bodies should be for theirs. I cannot lift five thousand pounds, and do not chastise myself for that. Just as I lift as much as I can when necessary, so I should reason as far and as effectively as I can, recognizing that the claims I make for what I come up with must always be guarded.

The seeming success of one kind of reasoning in science and technology has deluded many into expecting similar success elsewhere. There was a penchant for short-sighted complaints in the years immediately following the moon landings that took the general form, "If we can put a man on the moon, why can't we . . .?" Often, the blank was filled by some social problem like feeding the hungry.

Regrettably, the question is easily answered. Putting someone on the moon is almost infinitely easier than solving any problem involving the nature of human beings. Human nature is much further beyond our understanding and control than physical nature. Just a few of the factors in eliminating hunger that are not central problems in getting to the moon include indifference, greed, suspicion, insecurity, prejudice, fear, ignorance, and stubbornness. No Christian makes any greater leap of faith than does the typical liberal secularist who claims that a sufficient dose of reason (education) will rid us of these maladies. By comparison, hurtling someone to the moon is child's play.

If reason is severely limited, however, it is still usually preferable to its opposite. We have seen enough of the irrational in our world to understand the value of reason even with its flaws. What is dangerous is not the reasoning process, but unreasonable gullibility about its results. The process is morally and practically neutral, to be used like most things for good or for ill. Our own attitude toward reason and the use we make of it will determine the role it plays in our lives.

There is no more spurious use of reason than to suggest that reason demonstrates that faith in God is irrational. It simply is not so, and anyone who argues such does not understand the nature of reason or faith. They are also wrong, however, who claim that reason and evidence *prove* the existence of God. God is not reducible to proof and only our weakness makes us wish it were so.

It is my experience that, for all its usefulness in many areas, the closer one gets to the nexus where the eternal and temporal intersect, the less reason operates effectively as the primary instrument of judgment. In fact, reason recedes in importance in most of the truly critical areas of the human experience, largely because there are forces at work with which reason is not adequate to deal.

In our relationship with other human beings, in aesthetic expression and appreciation, in the spiritual realm, and in others having to do with essential human needs, the logical evaluation of objective evidence is peripheral to more important ways of understanding and acting. Reason is not usually the crucial component of one's love for another (overanalysis may actually weaken the love by turning the beloved into an object), or of one's response to a work of art (unless one has to explain—rationalize—the response), or of what one ultimately values in life.

Neither should it be the primary tool by which one evaluates a relationship to God—not because faith can't stand up to reason, as the secularist contends, but because reason is simply inadequate for the task. It has at best certain preliminary contributions to make in an area where its methodology, especially when operating alone, yields meager results. Making reason the primary arbiter in matters of faith ignores both the nature of the message (which is a person and a relationship, not an argument) and the nature of the recipient (who is also a person, not a computer).

This kind of talk is profoundly disturbing to those with a rationalist bent, whether Christian or secular. For the rationalistic Christian apologist (who, interestingly, is often anti-intellectual at the same time), such a position is a dead giveaway of imbibing in the existential, relativistic spirit of the times. (And attaching those names—existential, relativistic—to a position is usually felt to make it unnecessary to actually show why it is incorrect.) For the rationalistic secularist, it is mere primitivism of one kind or another.

It is not my intention, nor perhaps within my abilities, to delineate precisely where and how reason can and cannot be used. The view of reason I am putting forth neither denies its importance nor advocates a floating detachment from all truth claims. On the contrary, it makes commitment possible

where a false notion of reason might protest. Because I understand the inherent limitations of the reasoning process and
allow it only its legitimate role in relation to faith, I can justify
taking risks that carry me beyond the narrowness and illusory
safety of mere reason.

*   *   *   *   *

On the way home from the conference Alex made a mistake.
He thought it would be nice to look up a friend he hadn't
seen since high school. Alex had long been mildly maso-
chistic.

He remembered Annie fondly. He remembered her gentle
spirit and unsuspecting sincerity, and winced at recalling when
he and his friends had taken advantage of those qualities to
have some fun at her expense. Like the time they told her
the algebra teacher's son had died of food poisoning, and she
sent him a card expressing her sorrow.

Alex also remembered her as the girl who always carried
a Bible to school, right out where it could be seen. She used
to take a lot of kidding about it, but always smiled and said
something about it being her sword.

Alex had learned where Annie lived from another high
school companion a few months back. It was so close to his
route home from the conference that he felt it was providential
that he stop and see her. Such feelings should be resisted.

She was in the driveway unloading groceries from her car
as he came up.

"Goodness gracious, if it isn't Alex Adamson. What in the
world are you doing here?"

"Oh, just passing through and thought I'd renew an old
acquaintance along the way."

"Well isn't that sweet of you. It's great to see you. Come
on in the house and let's catch up on, what is it, the last ten
years or so."

Alex grabbed two bags of groceries and they headed in
through the front door. Annie pushed open the screen with

her foot and held it while Alex passed. He was greeted by a tropical array of climbers, clingers, creepers, and crawlers.

"Norman is into plants," Annie explained as Alex marveled at the elaborate woven contrivances in which many of the plants rested.

"Reminds me of *The Bridge Over the River Kwai.*"

"The what?" Annie asked as she set her load on the kitchen table.

"Never mind. So your husband's name is Norm."

Annie's voice tensed slightly. "No, I'm not married, Alex. Norman is my friend." She turned her back quickly and stuck her head in a bag of groceries.

Alex started to say, "I see," but quickly rejected that for "You don't say," which immediately made him wish he'd said, "I see." He recovered brilliantly, however, with "Are these dried banana chips in this bag here?"

Annie appeared thankful even for that question. "Yes, Norman is into health foods. He won't eat any processed food. It is very important to him to eat right. You'll be able to meet him in a few minutes. He always comes home for lunch since he can't get what he wants in restaurants and the law firm won't allow him to bring a sack lunch to work. I'm glad for that myself. It gives us a chance to visit in the middle of the day."

Her words were still in the air when the front screen door banged and Norm walked into the kitchen. The sight of a strange man in his kitchen startled him and he looked at Alex as though someone should begin an explanation quickly.

"Norman, this is Alex Adamson. He's an old friend from high school who just stopped by a couple of minutes ago. We haven't seen each other for ten years or more."

Norm looked as though the phrase "an old friend from high school" was too imprecise for his liking. It seemed he intended to regard Alex warily until he had more to go on.

"Nice to meet you, Alex. What brings you here after ten years?"

"Nothing really. I'm just on my way home from a conference, and I thought it would be nice to see somebody from the old days."

Annie leaped into the midst of the pleasantries. "What kind of conference, Alex? What is it you do?"

"I'm an English teacher."

Norm seemed to relax. Who could be threatened by somebody who spent his life amid gerunds and participles?

"Where do you teach?"

"At a small place up in the Cities called Redeemed College."

Norm was visibly relieved. He allowed himself to be cordial.

"Listen, Alex. Why don't you sit down and have lunch with Ann and I? I'd like to find out what she was like back in those days."

Alex said *"and me"* to himself, and "Thanks, I'd like that very much" to Norm.

As Annie washed and chopped the various leafy things that would constitute their lunch, Norm questioned Alex more closely about Redeemed. "Now what kind of place is this Redeemed College, Alex? Is it one of those TV preacher colleges? You know, one week they're telling you that God's ministry is going off the air unless people send in their tithes and offerings, and the next week they announce the opening of their new Christian university and hotel complex."

"Well, no. Redeemed apparently has been around for a while—since before television anyway. It was more likely built by tent meetings than television."

"Tent meetings? What's a tent meeting?"

"Never mind. It's not important."

"You know it amazes me that these places still exist. I can understand religion hanging on a while longer, but in places of supposedly higher learning—it just boggles the mind. How do you explain it, Alex?"

"Explain what? I'm not sure what you're talking about exactly." Alex knew only too well what he was talking about and couldn't help thinking how much closer to home he would be if he had just stayed on the freeway.

"I mean what do they do with science at a place like that,

or with psychology or anthropology or almost anything discovered in the last 150 years? What do they do with Freud and Einstein and Ayn Rand?"

"Ayn Rand?"

"You know what I mean. Religion has been bankrupt since the middle of the nineteenth century. Are people still trying to resurrect the body?"

Mixed metaphor, Alex thought to himself. Unfortunately that's all he could think of. He couldn't think of a good place to begin to try to answer the man's question, which seemed suspiciously more like a statement than a question anyway. Lawyering had taught him the art of making assertions while seeming to be asking questions.

"Well, it's hard to know where to begin. I guess I don't see any contradiction between faith and reason, if that's what you mean." There was a good start. The compatibility of faith and reason. One couldn't ask for a firmer truism on which to build his defense. Unfortunately, Norm didn't know enough to leave a good truism alone.

"Why don't you see a contradiction?"

"What?"

"I said, why don't you see a contradiction?"

"Well, I just don't."

"You don't see a contradiction between believing in a good, all-powerful God and a billion starving people? You don't see a contradiction between Christian pronouncements and the death of six million Jews at the hands of a Christian nation? You don't see a contradiction between Genesis and Darwin?" Norm was gathering momentum. Annie tried to divert his attention.

"Norman, is it all right if I mix these onions with the greens before frying them?"

Norm was genuinely pained. "Ann, I've told you before that the onions give off lectatic acid when they are cooking, which kills the vitamin A in the greens if they are cooked together. Cook them separately and then mix them together afterward."

He turned back to Alex, who had used the brief moment trying to figure out what C. S. Lewis would have done in this situation.

"Listen, Alex. I don't want to hassle you. If you want to believe all that stuff it's your business. I guess it just bothers me when I think of whole schools of young people being indoctrinated into that stuff. I mean, these people are dangerous. They are looking for simplistic answers to real problems in our society. They're trying to return us to the Middle Ages where you had the castle and the cathedral and everybody else out in the fields. It's like Ann, here. When I first met her five years ago she was just like that."

"Norman, please. Don't bring me into this."

"Oh don't worry. Alex knew you in high school. He must have known you were into religion then."

"I wasn't 'into religion,' Norman. I believed things then that I can't believe anymore, but. . . . Oh never mind. You never did understand."

"I understand perfectly well, Ann. I was a religion minor in college, I'll remind you. I learned more of the truth about Christianity in one 'World Religions' course than you did in twenty years of Bible studies and pious sermons."

Alex's thoughts were not respectful. ("The guy probably cut half the classes and read just enough to wing it on the essay questions. And with this sterling background he's going to make pronouncements on the things of heaven and earth.")

"I'm not some ignorant pagan, you know. And one thing that I understand is that it took me two years to get you to join the twentieth century."

Annie seemed hurt and embarrassed to have something that was clearly very painful to her paraded out for lunchtime conversation. Alex saw the same gentleness and vulnerability that he had remembered.

"There are some things in the twentieth century that I'd just as soon not join up with."

"Well you can't pick and choose my dear. The world is what it is, and it won't do any good to pretend it's something else. What about you, Alex? You seem like an intelligent enough fellow. How do you explain people getting polio shots on the one hand and praying to a slightly revamped version of Zeus on the other? Do you know what I mean?"

Alex wished he didn't. He felt like saying something about casting pearls before swine, but thought Norm might get hung up on the swine part and miss the point. Where did you start to answer such a question, put in such a way? It was hard enough to know where to start in explaining it to yourself. Do you tell him that even as a child you had a clear sense of your own sinfulness? That the apostle Paul or the writer of Ecclesiastes seem to you to have understood human nature better than Freud? That everything you saw in the twentieth century only confirmed for you the biblical account of the human condition? That sometimes you *couldn't* explain it and weren't even sure you believed anything anymore—but that somehow that seemed all right with God? He could start anywhere and yet he could start nowhere. He settled for being insipid.

"Well, that's a tough question. I guess different people just see things differently. Faith is sort of a personal thing, you know, that's sort of hard to explain."

"True enough. Like I say. If that's where you're at, that's fine. I've got no problem with religious people. I play racquetball with a guy every week who's in charge of his church's building drive. As long as they don't try to push their beliefs down everyone else's throats, they have as much right to their opinions as anyone else."

Norm beamed across the table, awash in the afterglow of his magnanimity. Alex smiled back, trying his best to look like someone who wouldn't dream of shoving anything down anyone's throat. Annie set a bowl of steaming vegetation between them, her eyes filled with tears and a look of anguish on her face.

*   *   *   *   *

The goal of both reason and faith, as we have seen, is truth, a universal virtue sought by all in one way or another and by no one more than the reflective Christian. Both by temperament and conviction, reflective Christians are truth-seekers. They pursue it passionately; they grieve over its elusiveness. The truth claims of Christianity are likely to be very important to their faith, and the sham and hypocrisy in institutional religion will therefore pain them greatly.

This desire for truth makes reflective Christians susceptible to a very widespread confusion in our culture—the confusion of *truth* with *certainty*. The ruling methodology for reaching truth in much of the secular culture, also very influential in some religious spheres, reflects the dominance of the scientific model. Essentially, one amasses evidence—as analyzed, classified, and approved by reason—guarding at all times against methodological lapses (like subjective bias, logical fallacy, faulty or misinterpreted data), until one reaches something very like certainty, until one has *proof.*

Now professional philosophers and other academics will readily admit, even insist, that absolute certainty of course is not attainable. And much secular truth-seeking will in fact violate this method even as it pretends to follow it. Still, the feeling is very widespread that the goal of reasoning is certainty and that, if we can simply think clearly and logically enough, we can solve our individual and collective problems and get on with the business of being happy.

In the most important matters of life, as I have argued, this approach has only limited usefulness. There are simply too many variables, too much that is incalculable or non-rational, in short *too much humanness* involved for this method to work conclusively.

Unfortunately, much of the church has also sold out to the myth of certainty. One kind of Christian apologetic claims certainty based on faith, another on a combination of faith and a rationalistic analysis of evidence. Their ultimate goal is the same: an unquestionable, undoubtable foundation on which to base all subsequent claims.

"We don't have to float around like the poor secularist," we are told by the rationalistic Christian, "because we have absolutes. The secularist lost his absolutes when he got rid of God. Because God is our absolute, our truth claims are certain, not contingent; objective, not subjective; eternal, not temporal." The careful Christian apologist realizes that belief in absolutes is just that, a belief (and justifiable as such, I hasten to add), but the typical Christian in the pew is left with the distinct impression that absolutes give us certainty about the things of faith.

In order to promote this feeling of certainty, conservative Christendom erects an elaborate system of apologetics, group psychology (each feeds off the certainty the other supposedly has), and, often, legalism. Even the reflective person often succumbs to the false either-or of institutional belief: "Either you have the certainty about God and His will that we do, or you are possibly not even a believer at all." As a result, many either try to "believe harder," seeking the tranquil unquestioning that seems the ideal, or, out of a sense of confused integrity, sever themselves from the church whose standard they cannot meet.

Make no mistake, this approach to truth is enormously powerful and attractive. Our appetite for certainty has only grown in our troubled century. The further away it is, the more desirable it seems. Who would not want this kind of certainty if it were available? As insecurity threatens on so many fronts, the man who offers a guarantee with faith will attract a large and devoted following. He will appear, not without reason, as a man of conviction, a prophet, a defender of the faith against forces of evil.

And how will the question-asker appear by comparison? What of our poor, reflective Christian, struggling to believe, lamenting his disbelief? He or she will appear weak, irresolute, wishy-washy. He will inspire no confidence, attract no following, earn no respect—not even his own. He or she may envy the people for whom the world divides neatly into good and evil, God and Satan, elect and damned. He may wonder at their confidence, their sense of purpose, their freedom from tormenting doubts, but, whether he desires these things or not, the workings of his mind put such untroubled confidence out of reach.

Ironically, the insistence on certainty destroys its very possibility. The demand for certainty inevitably *creates* its opposite—doubt. Doubt derives its greatest strength from those who fear it most. Unwisely glorified as the primary way to truth by many secularists, it is equally unwisely feared by many in Christendom as truth's mortal enemy.

Books and preachers aplenty counsel about dealing with, which usually means getting rid of, doubt. The pious Christian version of Abraham often turns him into an automaton. God says, "Sacrifice your son Isaac to me." Abraham, eyes glazed, mind dormant, body stiff, says in a slow, robotic monotone, "Yes, Master. Whatever you say, Master." This, for many in and outside the church, is the Christian view of faith.

Was Abraham, to change the metaphor, an Old Testament Steppin Fetchit, holding his hat obsequiously in hand? Didn't he, rather, gape at the enormity of it? Didn't he argue, plead, question, object? Are we to believe nothing took place between the command in verse 2 of Genesis 22 and the departure for the sacrificial mountain in verse 3? Is Abraham a greater or lesser man, a greater or lesser example of faith, if we suppose he received the command calmly?

T. S. Eliot sees a certain kind of doubt as inevitable in matters of faith and correctly suggests that one's *attitude* toward doubt is more significant than one's having doubt: "Every man who thinks and lives by thought must have his own skepticism . . . that which ends in denial, or that which leads to faith and which is somehow integrated into the faith which transcends it." [1] The notion of transcending doubt by accepting it *into* faith, rather than by suppressing it (for it can never be destroyed), is crucial. Perhaps doubt, rather than something to be crushed, can be made to serve faith.

Doubt can only be robbed of its paralyzing and destructive

qualities when it is admitted for what it is—which isn't nearly as much as it appears when not admitted—and is accounted for in the process of faith. Normally doubt is seen as sapping faith's strength. Why not the reverse? Where there is doubt, faith has its reason for being. Clearly faith is not needed where certainty supposedly exists, but only in situations where doubt is possible, even present.

Do I doubt when I look at the pain in the world that there can be a good God hovering behind, in, and through it? Fine, this gives tested faith (not blind wishful thinking) a place to operate. As I live and interpret my experiences through the eyes of faith, doubt is not replaced by certainty—I can still be broken by the suffering I see everywhere—but faith puts it in its place. Doubt makes its claims, even daily, and they are respected, but they do not determine the character of my life.

Thus far I have had in mind primarily doubts about the things of God. I should mention, at least in passing, doubts about the pronouncements of men and women. Some doubts are God-given. Though overvalued as the methodological key to truth in our culture, doubting can at times protect us from many assertions—religious and secular—which richly deserve to be doubted.

* * * * *

Mr. Slayer was a short man. *That explained part of it right there,* Alex thought—*short men compensating for feelings of inferiority with aggressive behavior: Napoleon, Hitler, Rumpelstiltskin, most of your mass murderers.* As loath to change his hairstyle as his theology, Slayer's thinning and well-oiled hair was a repudiation of the new generation of blow-dried evangelists.

Slayer fidgeted in his seat on the platform as the President droned through his introductory remarks. Like an athlete awaiting the start of the contest, he was filled with an excess of energy, anxious to begin the struggle.

The President was up to his usual tricks, trying to appropri-

ate to himself and the college any glory the speaker might
have brought with him. These evening meetings were more
for the local community than for the students, and the President was making the most of his self-confessed public relations
skills. After three or four references to "my friend," he let
out a final "my very good friend" and stepped back, confident
that whatever might follow, he had done his part extraordinar-
ily well.

Mr. Slayer walked single-mindedly to the microphone, shak-
ing the hand of the retreating President. He stood quietly for
just a moment, gathering himself, his eyes averted down and
to the side. He had no notes of any kind. The audience was
reverent, and finally he spoke.

"I'm angry." He paused. "I'm very angry." He looked up
for the first time. "And I pray to God you are too. If you
are not angry, I'd like to know why." He swept a knee-weaken-
ing look from one side to the other. "How can you not be
angry? Are you living in the same world I am? Do you love
the same God I love? Do your eyes work? Do your ears work?
Or are you Helen Keller Christians?"

What an opening, Alex thought to himself. *This is panzer
preaching. Hit them fast, hard, and often. This fellow doesn't
fool around. Calls for a long pass on the first play of the game.*

"If you do have eyes and ears and you've kept them open
like I have, then they're probably filled with garbage. Ladies
and gentlemen, our society is filled with the vilest kind of
trash, and it's growing ranker every day. And I'm here to
tell you that if we don't start doing some trash disposal we
are going to be buried in it. Everything we love, everything
we value, will be gone and we'll wonder where it went.

"What kind of trash am I talking about? I'll tell you just
a few of the varieties I have in mind. I'm talking about the
muck that oozes from our television sets. That's right—the
big eye, the household god that is sitting on its altar in your
home right now as you listen to my voice. At this very minute,
many of your children are worshiping at that altar. And what
is the order of service? Sex, violence, perversion, anti-church

and anti-American propaganda, materialism, immorality of every kind, and emptiness. That's the kind of trash I'm talking about.

"What kind of trash am I talking about? I'm talking about the trash that flows out of our legislative bodies. I'm talking about social legislation which, under the guise of compassion and concern, is turning our country into a socialist state. When was the last time somebody paid *you* for doing nothing?" Alex wondered if anyone thought of farmers when he said that. "How long do you think the family will last when we allow people to deduct childcare from their taxes? Childcare my foot! I call it 'childcare-less.' Any woman who would dump her child into one of those baby bins so she and hubby can drive matching Maseratis couldn't care less about her child. Childcare-less, that's what it is."

It was coming fast. Alex tried to sort out the assertions and assumption in just the last few sentences, but more was on the way.

"In Sweden now, you *have* to put your children in daycare. There's no choice. The way they've set up the tax laws, you have to turn your child over to the state. And when the state has the children, don't you see, they have everything. Everything! That's the kind of trash I'm talking about."

Why does Sweden always get it from these guys? Alex wondered. *Little country trying to mind its own business, and it's second only to Russia in its offense to fundamentalist, capitalist sensibilities. Pornography and socialism—surely there's more to the country than that.*

"What kind of trash am I talking about? I'm talking about the trash that tumbles from the highest court in our land. I'm talking about not letting our precious little ones pray to their Maker at the beginning of the school day. Oh, if that doesn't break your heart, my friends, then you have no heart to break. I'm talking about rushing to protect the rights of criminals while the helpless victim is still lying bleeding in the gutter. I'm talking about attempts to keep us from arming ourselves for the protection of our own homes and families while drug-crazed killers stalk our streets. That's the kind of trash I'm talking about."

He paused now for the first time in what had been an uninterrupted stream of passionate declamation. He allowed the silence to last long enough that the crowd ached to hear the next word. He started again slowly, his words pronounced quietly and carefully but portending greater things, as an ocean swell gathers slowly but inexorably in its mounting movement toward the thunderous shore.

"But all this, my friends, is as nothing. It doesn't even deserve our attention. It is the mere buzzing of a fly compared to the enormity of an offense that I haven't even mentioned. You know what I'm talking about. And are you going to sit there and tell me you aren't angry? You aren't angry about this stench that rises to the nostrils of God? In the Old Testament the Jewish people sacrificed the best of their flocks to God to send up to Him a sweet savor on the winds of heaven.

"What are we sending up, ladies and gentlemen? What sacrifice is the United States of America making in our day? Babies! Babies! One million five hundred thousand babies, sacrificed every year at the altar of selfishness! One million five hundred thousand little girls and boys sacrificed at the altar of family planning! One million five hundred thousand Americans sacrificed every year so that women can control their own bodies!

"Control their own bodies? If most of them had controlled their own bodies, they wouldn't have gotten pregnant in the first place. And what about the poor infant's body? What about that body that the Psalmist tells us God personally knit in the womb of that mother? What are we to say about that little body, at whatever stage of its development, when it is burned with that caustic saline solution? What about that body when it is cut up in parts so it can be vacuumed out of the mother's womb like so much debris under a sofa? Who is going to stick up for that body, for that precious little baby?

"I'll tell you who—no one. No one is going to help that baby, those one and a half million babies every year. No one is going to lift a finger—unless it's us. Unless it's you and unless it's me. Because I'll tell you something, my friends. I'll tell you something Christian father. I'll tell you something Christian mother. I'll tell you something Christian young man and young woman—secular humanists don't care two cents about human life. Secular humanists will not protect the sanctity of life because they have no reason to. They haven't any reason in the world to care about human life, and the more logical they are the more they realize that.

"Why do I say that? Aren't some humanists good people? Sure, there are humanists who sincerely want to do the right thing. But, my friends, they haven't got a snowball's chance in hell of doing the right thing for more than five minutes at a time because they have cut themselves off from the source of all that is right and good—almighty God and His Son, Jesus Christ.

"Humanism is a house built on shifting sand. It has no foundation. Any regard it has for human life is a sentimental holdover from the time when our society was based on the bedrock of Christian morality. But that sentimentality has all but washed away, ladies and gentlemen. There is only a faint residue of respect for life left. Our society has convinced itself that a baby before it is born is just an insignificant blob of protoplasm, spared or destroyed at the whim of any girl or woman who might find a child inconvenient. That was the first big hurdle. It took years to jump it. The rest will be easy."

The sweat was now heavy on his brow, and he made no attempt to wipe it away. "If a baby that is undesirable before birth can be eliminated, why not shortly after birth, especially if it isn't perfect? That is happening right now, my friends. Not in the future—now! And if we can get rid of babies, should we really spend all this money to take care of the retarded? After all, it's the quality of life that counts, they tell us. Mere biological life isn't enough. And can we seriously think the retarded have quality lives? Preposterous. Clearly they must go!"

The sarcasm in his voice was matched by the growing anger

in the faces of the audience. "And while we are tidying up our society, have you noticed how many old people there are? They are really starting to clutter things up. These people have the right to die with dignity, don't you think? It's only right that we help them fulfill this right. Many of them apparently are so senile that they think they want to keep living. Such obvious senility clearly is not consistent with the kind of quality of life these people deserve. We must help them correct this problem by putting an end to their obvious suffering.

"Do you think I'm exaggerating, my friends? Oh would to God I was exaggerating. Wouldn't I be the happiest man in the world to find that I'd made all this up, that it wasn't true, that it's all just a bad dream, that I'll wake up to find my country once again the land of the free, the home of the brave, the protector of the weak. Where, oh where, my friends, did we go wrong? How has this come upon a country that was founded on the Bible, by Bible-believing men of God?

"I'll tell you this. It didn't come all at once. It came slowly but ever so surely in little steps, one after the other. It came when we said a man no longer had to work to eat. It came when we joined a world organization where godless countries insult and harass us on our own soil—while we pay them to do it. It came when we kicked God out of our schools. It came when we didn't kick the communists out of Korea or Vietnam. It came when we adopted a 'do-it-if-it-feels-good' morality. It came when television put the toilet in the living room."

He was covered in perspiration now. He took out a handkerchief, unfolded it, and deliberately wiped his face, leaving the audience to chew on the bones he had thrown them. When he finished, he slowly refolded the handkerchief and calmly began again.

"I don't need to tell you people this. You have eyes and ears to see and hear. You are witnesses to the tragedy of our society. Unfortunately, that's not the end of the bad news, I'm afraid. That's not even the worst of it. I wish it were. I wish I could stand here and tell you that the church, at least, is standing for God and country, that our Christian colleges are mighty fortresses for our God, a bulwark never failing. Oh, I wish I could tell you that, but it isn't so, and maybe this is something you haven't been aware of. While your eyes have been trained on the humanist enemy ahead, perhaps you haven't noticed that the enemy is also standing by your side, may in fact be sitting amongst us at this very moment. This may be the saddest part of the whole story. This may be where we must be, in God's name, the angriest.

"We all know the liberal church abandoned God long ago, and He them. Liberalism and neo-orthodoxy have been with us for many decades. But now the infection has spread to the Bible-believing churches. The fetching face of humanism has wooed and won the hearts and minds of many within our own ranks—and not just among the enlistees, but in the highest reaches of the Christian army.

"Let me give you just a few examples. Take *The Christian World,* that supposed flagship magazine of evangelical Christianity. For ten years I've been waiting for a hard-hitting stand against humanism from this so-called Christian publication. For ten years I've looked for them to launch an assault on the godless philosophy from the pit of hell that is destroying everything around us. Two months ago they finally devoted a whole issue to humanism. And what did we get? The most wishy-washy, weak-willed, namby-pamby pile of garbage I've ever seen. It is enough to make you sick. Get a load of the title of the lead article—'Humanism: Pro and Con.' Did you hear that, pro and con? They had one simpering fellow criticizing humanism, in the politest of terms I assure you, and another wolf-in-sheep's-clothing telling us how if we just understood what humanism was, we wouldn't think it was so bad. Oh, didn't Satan throw a party in hell celebrating that issue. 'It's so complicated,' they tell us. 'If you look at it from another perspective . . .' they tell us. I'll tell you something, friends. I'm only interested in one perspective and that's God's perspective. And, as far as I'm concerned, God wrote 'Ichabod' across that magazine's masthead with that issue, if he hadn't already done so long before."

This was too wonderful for mere listening. The crowd burst into applause as one. Slayer showed no pleasure in their approval, his expression becoming only fiercer, as if his indignation fed on the sound of appreciation.

"And if it were only in our publications, perhaps it wouldn't be so bad. What godly man reads those anyway? But it is also in our Christian schools and colleges—the places we trust to educate our children. Would it shock you to know that the theory of evolution is being openly taught in some of our Christian colleges? Have you ever met a biologist who says he believes in both creation *and* evolution? I have. Have you ever met an English teacher who called himself a Christian humanist? I have. At a Christian college! You figure that one out for me—a Christian humanist. Next thing you know we'll have Christian satanists and democratic communists and God knows what.

"Don't you see, people, that even language has been destroyed? That abortion becomes 'terminated pregnancy,' that socialism is called 'concern for the poor,' that the attempt to make us helpless before atheistic communism is called a 'peace movement'? Where will this all end?

"I'll tell you where it will end if you and I don't get angry and do something about it. It will end with Christians either in chains or with the mark of the beast on their foreheads. It will end when they march down the center aisle of our churches to arrest the preacher—if there are any left who haven't sold out. It will end when getting caught with a Bible will cost you your life. It will end when they are mixing birth control pills in the lunches of high school kids.

"What can we do about it? How can we turn back this tide of filth and sickness? I don't have time to go into great detail right now, but it's all in my book, *Sweeping Clean the Temple,* which is on sale out in the lobby after the meeting.

"Let me suggest a few things, however. First, we must get on our knees. An army dare not go into battle without ammunition, nor a Christian into battle without prayer. Second, this is a battle that is being fought on many fronts. In our society we must fight fire with fire. Organize! Participate in the political process. We fundamentalists have been contemplating our spiritual navels while the humanists have been taking over society through the ballot box. They're immoral as sin, but you can't accuse them of being illegal. So where are we? Don't we also have the right to vote, to petition, to lobby?

"Oh, don't those liberals screech when they see us beating them at their own game! Listen to them talk about the outrage of mixing religion and politics! Did you hear them complain about preachers marching during the civil rights movement? Did they wail about separation of church and state when liberal pastors marched against the Vietnam war? No, no—it's only when you try to protect the unborn, or want your children to pray in school that they suddenly decide religion should have nothing to do with politics. We can change things, ladies and gentlemen. Elect godly men whose vote will reflect their Christian convictions.

"But there is a fight within the church as well. Ferret out those corrupted by humanism within the body. Deal with them lovingly but without vacillation. Praise God that a sister institution of yours had the courage to dismiss a Bible professor who raised questions about the inerrancy of Scripture. Another so-called Christian college, however, employs a history professor who testified before Congress *against* the school prayer movement. To my knowledge, he has not been fired or even disciplined."

Slayer looked back over his shoulder at the President whose own eyes had been moist with emotion for some time. "This is something you may want to take up, Mr. President, with your counterpart at that sister institution." The President looked appropriately aggrieved and nodded vigorously.

"This is unpleasant business, but it must be done. A house divided against itself cannot stand. Scripture tells us if your eye offends thee, pluck it out. The body of Christ, my friends, has some diseased parts that must be surgically removed lest the infection spread. I hope to be able to carry away a good report about Redeemed College to your many supporters as I travel around the country.

"It is a time for examination. God winnowed Gideon's army until only the pure in heart remained. This is not a time for compromisers. How does one compromise with the Devil? It is a time for anger—for righteous, holy anger. It is a time for the people of God to stand up and be counted. Who is on the Lord's side? Thank you, ladies and gentlemen, for your kind attention—and God bless you all."

Whether to be counted or not, stand up they did. The applause was so loud that Alex felt it in his chest as well as with his ears. He wasn't much for standing ovations, but then why be the only one sitting in an auditorium full of people, especially angry ones on the lookout for signs of corruption? He stood with the others, applauding circumspectly. There was an excess of emotion in their faces, not of happiness to be sure, but more like a grim satisfaction at this verification that things were as bad as they thought.

The President was beaming on stage, obviously thrilled by the undeniable success of the occasion. He kept applauding with the others as he walked to where Slayer stood a few feet away from the microphone. He grabbed Slayer's hand with both his own and pumped his arm mercilessly. Slayer seemed not to notice. His eyes stared off into the rafters, intent, as though seeking out enemies as yet undiscovered.

* * * * *

What then of the "absolutes" which form the foundation for a popular kind of Christian apologetic? Might not absolutes be an avenue to certainty and freedom from doubt? Surely this approach deserves consideration. We wouldn't want to miss its benefits if true, nor to embrace it, no matter how satisfying, if less than true. That it runs counter to the drift of thought in our time is, when one considers our time, probably in its favor. The dominating point of view—that all values, beliefs, and outlooks are self-manufactured in response to environmental pressures—is not overwhelmingly attractive.

The apologetic based on the notion of absolutes generally argues that the qualities of God—His transcendence, omnipotence, eternality, and so on—put the things of God in stark contrast to the immanent, limited, and transient world of humanity. The things of God, therefore, form absolutes, ultimates, universal and unchanging verities which human beings can appropriate to build their lives on. Such absolutes, for the Christian, include God's existence, His love for His creation, and the redeeming work of Jesus Christ.

Few Christians would question the centrality of these things. They are the heart of faith, the reason for risking everything if only they be true. But what are we to make of this concept of absolutes as the basis for belief and commitment? In one form or another, every Christian has asked, "How can I know for sure? Do I dare to base my only life on this?" Do absolutes provide the answer to these questions? Can the demon of doubt be crushed once and for all?

With typical reflective decisiveness, my answer is no—and yes. A naive conception of absolutes offers a truth packaged in an illusion accompanied by a danger. The truth, which I affirm by faith in response to evidence, is that the essential Christian claims are actually so. The illusion is that I can be certain that they are so. The danger is that my eventual discovery that certainty is an illusion (one that never should have been offered in the first place) may lead me, mistakenly, to disavow the truth it enveloped.

The idea of knowing absolutes has a very limited meaning at best when it is human beings who are the supposed knowers. Absolutes, by definition, partake of infinity; they are without boundary. What relationship can a finite knower have with an infinite object of knowledge except a finite, limited one? Can one then be said to know or "have" an absolute on which to ground one's beliefs when one only knows, at best, a sliver of that absolute?

One knows something, to be sure, but is it an absolute?

How could we know it was an absolute unless our knowledge encompassed the whole? Someone standing on the shore of an ocean may think, as people perhaps once did, "This water goes on forever—it is infinite." But how would we know unmistakably that anything was infinite or absolute unless we ourselves were infinite?

Furthermore, as fallen creatures, our knowledge of any absolute is not only partial, it is distorted. Even if by some stretch of the imagination we could extrapolate the infinite from the finite, arguing that partial knowledge of an absolute demonstrates the existence of the whole, we confront the claim of Christian orthodoxy itself that all our perceptions are at least partially *flawed* as well as limited. It only rubs salt in the wound to point out how those who claim absolutes as the basis for faith draw greatly divergent, even contradictory, conclusions from the same absolutes.

Even this brief consideration suggests, to me at least, that a doctrine of absolutes offers little for raising the level of certainty or eradicating the specter of doubt for the reflective Christian. Does this mean the radical pluralist is right? Not necessarily. My inability to know any absolute absolutely does not prove such things do not exist, only that my limited knowledge of them is not grounds for certainty.

It is equally unjustifiable to proclaim God unknowable. There is a vast difference between saying our knowledge of God is always partial, flawed, slanted by personal and cultural idiosyncrasies, and asserting there is nothing beyond ourselves even to know. The reflective Christian must steer between unfounded claims of certainty on the one hand and an equally spurious absolutizing of relativism on the other.

As an illustration, assume that I go to a football game with 50,000 other people. Clearly each of us experiences the game differently; no one even *sees* the same game. There are so many different aspects of the game occurring simultaneously that I can see only bits and pieces. One person watches mostly the quarterback, another focuses on the line play, a third is preoccupied with the cheerleaders. Even if a thousand people are all watching one player, they are doing so from different locations in the stadium, with differing degrees of acuity of eyesight, or of understanding of what they are seeing.

The spectators' experiences differ greatly in other respects as well. The game is going to seem different to me if someone behind me is constantly screaming, or spills beer on my head. A myriad of other factors like how I got along with my wife this morning, unconscious worries about my job, and the like all impinge to make my experience, and everyone else's, unique.

Our experience of "absolutes" is something like our experience of this game. Just as no one fully experiences the game, so no one comprehends an absolute. Presence at the game does not guarantee that one sees it truthfully, as it "really" happened. (Did he step on the line? More verifiable. Was that the correct strategy? Less verifiable.) In one sense, there were as many "games" played as there were spectators and participants.

One must insist on the significance, however, that there was, in fact, a football game played—in time and space—and that it was not a mass illusion. The problem with the absolutists is not that they insist that there was a football game (and that there are absolutes), but that some insist reason dictates that only their view of the game (east end zone, row seventy-five) is correct. Equally suspect, however, is the person who argues that since we all had different views of the game, and cannot agree on precisely what happened, then there wasn't a game (or absolutes) at all, that everyone created a mythical game in response to personal need.

The notion of absolutes is a *human* attempt to explain the ways of God to ourselves (not, by the way, the approach used in biblical revelation), just as our desire for certainty is part of a very human longing for security. To say they are human is not to condemn them. I do not use the word *merely,* as many do, when describing things they do not approve of: merely human, merely subjective, merely emotional, and so on. Why dismiss legitimate human qualities and longings as though they deserve contempt?

Whether by invoking faith or absolutes or human reason or, ironically, by claiming all belief is illusory, many people pursue the myth of certainty. I call it a myth because that is my understanding of it. If you feel you have certainty, I have no desire to convince you otherwise. God bless you in your certainty. But many, like Pascal, have found it incompatible with human experience. My own experience is that for human beings certainty does not exist, has never existed, will not—in our finite states—ever exist, and, moreover, should not. It is not a gift God has chosen to give His creatures, doubtlessly wisely.

Pascal felt keenly this human dilemma of having enough knowledge to awaken our appetites without having enough to satisfy them. One passage among many from *Pensées* that reflect this painful circumstance summarizes much of what I have been trying to say in the first half of this book:

> This is our true state; this is what makes us incapable of certain knowledge and of absolute ignorance. We sail within a vast sphere, ever drifting in uncertainty, driven from end to end. When we think to attach ourselves to any point . . . it wavers and leaves us. . . . Nothing stays for us. This is our natural condition, and yet most contrary to our inclination; we burn with desire to find solid ground and an ultimate sure foundation whereon to build a tower reaching to the Infinite. But our whole groundwork cracks, and the earth opens to abysses.
>
> Let us therefore not look for certainty and stability. Our reason is always deceived by fickle shadows. . . .[2]

It is, I hope, already clear that while I believe this to be a compelling description of the condition into which we are born, I (with Pascal) do not believe it to be our inescapable end. While certainty is beyond our reach, *meaning*—something far more valuable—is not. Meaning derives from a right relationship with God, based not on certainty and conformity, but on risk and commitment.

5
The Risk of Commitment

*We must know where to doubt, where to feel
certain, where to submit. He who does not
do so, understands not the force of reason.*
—*Pascal*

*The highest of all is not to understand the highest
but to act upon it.*
—*Kierkegaard*

*The noncommitted have no right to ask
any questions.*
—*Helmut Thielicke*

BEING HUMAN IS A RISKY BUSINESS. This is a basic, undisputed truth. Our bodies are subject to every kind of calamity. Our minds and spirits struggle, sometimes unsuccessfully, with the enormous task of making sense out of our experiences. At every point we are confronted with the breach between the longings of our heart and the limits of our situation.

No significant area of life is free from risk. It is a key ingredient in every accomplishment and every relationship. Whenever a decision is required, there is risk. Wherever we must act, there is risk. Wherever people intertwine their lives, there is risk. Should we expect it to be any different in our relationship with transcendence? Why should we insist on being certain about God, on having proof of His existence, or on having unmistakable absolutes on which to build a faith when none of these is compatible with being the finite creatures God has created?

If risk is an inescapable part of the daily life of the businessman or woman, the politician, the farmer, the artist, if it is at the heart of all meaningful relationships between people, then we should not be chagrined or embarrassed to find it also at the heart of a relationship with God. Believers have always been risk-takers (how else does one explain Abraham or Bonhoeffer?). Perhaps it's because God Himself has been a risk-taker; witness His decision to create humankind and then to make Himself one with us.

Accepting the riskiness of faith entails confronting the possibility of being wrong. That any one person is in error in some part of his or her conception of the life of faith is inevitable, but the larger question is whether the whole enterprise of faith in God is fundamentally mistaken. There is no religious impulse or experience of any kind for which a totally nonreligious accounting cannot be constructed. The task at which reason excels is providing alternative explanations, and all religious experience can be explained away in terms of individual and group psychology, cultural conditioning, even brain physiology. Every phenomenon—religious, scientific, or whatever—is subject to multiple explanations, and people believe what they do based on many factors.

The reflective Christian does well, in my view, to freely admit this possibility of being wrong. All I believe may in fact be false. God may be only wish fulfillment. The sense of His presence that I sometimes get in worship and prayer may derive simply from the release of certain chemicals in the brain. Those occasions where He seems to have guided my life may only be coincidence or reflect my human desire to find a pattern in events.

But then again, all that I believe regarding God and Christ may be essentially true. Reality may, in fact, be largely what the Christian faith claims it to be. The point is that risk is unavoidable either way. My faith in God does not provide certainty that He exists or is worthy of devotion (no matter how strongly I may feel about the matter), but this lack of certainty is not unique to the believer. The secularist takes an enormous risk in building a life that assumes that God is not central to things. The Christian should neither seek to deny the risk inherent in faith nor accept the implication that the secularist is on surer ground.

Many like to think they act on what they *know* while the believer merely wishes and hopes. In fact, everyone exercises some kind of faith daily that goes far beyond irrefutable evidence. If, as T. S. Eliot claims, we all carry a certain skepticism with us, then it is also true that we all exercise belief. Human life is not compatible with total disbelief. On the mundane level, we show incredible faith each time we drive down the road that everyone will stay on his own side of the little white line. Few things are as ridiculous as the person who claims not to believe in anything.

A fellow of my acquaintance held forth eloquently about the unknowability and likely nonexistence of God, the obvious childishness of religion, and the duty of thinking people to admit they know and believe in nothing. How passionate he became, however, on the subject of additives in food—health food versus junk food, organic versus processed, suspected conspiracies in high places. In doing so, he let slip his tentative speculations about reincarnation, though quickly adding, lest he be accused of believing something, that he wasn't sure. Clearly this fellow *believed* many things, much on the flimsiest evidence. He had simply avoided the risk of significant beliefs for the illusory safety of trivial ones.

Faith is a quality and a choice consistent with the riskiness of the human condition. It is an appropriate response to the world as I find it. It is a superior response to cynicism or despair which use the genuine difficulty of life to deny the very real opportunity for discovering meaning in it. Faith is likewise not so weak a thing that it can exist only where there is certainty and proof, where there is no opposition either from within or without.

There is no more honest expression of the tension of faith than that of the distraught father in the gospel of Mark seeking healing for his child. To Jesus' assertion that belief makes all things possible, the father cries out in tears, "Lord, I believe; help thou my unbelief" (KJV). The New English Bible renders the verse, "I have faith, . . . help me where faith falls short." Surely this is the cry of many a reflective Christian. Surely this is the cry of Pascal, who simultaneously sees too much of God in the world to deny Him but too little to be sure beyond a doubt. One option is surrender to the paralyzing ambivalence of cautious uncertainty; another is to use uncertainty itself as a stepping stone to the risk of commitment.

In a cynical and relativistic age such as ours, the problem of commitment extends far beyond the world of religious faith. How can a thinking person with a keen, sometimes crushing, awareness of the complexity and contingency of all things make passionate commitment to act in the service of any contested cause? Do not the committed people in our society often seem those least sensitive to the complexity of things, least willing to grant any virtue or insight to holders of opposing views? This seems an age of extremists. Anyone in the middle looks wishy-washy, irresolute, hesitant. In oft-quoted lines brooding on the future of modern civilization, W. B. Yeats observes, "The best lack all conviction/While the worst are full of passionate intensity." One could well substitute "the reflective" in the first line and "the single-minded" in the second.

Typically, the reflective person is not instinctively a man or woman of action. As we have seen, reflection by its nature delays the moment of choice on which action depends. The typical person of action is blessed, in a sense, by seeing things simply. Those in business or the military, for instance, cannot allow themselves to be paralyzed by all the possibilities for failure that exist in any plan. They consider the available information for a relatively brief time, make a decision, and see that it is carried out. Our society's appreciation for this kind of person may explain the fondness in the church for business and military organizational models and figures of speech. We respect people who know their minds and get things done. "Damn the torpedoes, full speed ahead!"

Is Kierkegaard correct, then, when he says that reflection is usually the death of passion? Where is the balance point between necessary and realistic awareness of complexity on the one hand and hiding behind diversity, pluralism, and relativism as an excuse for moral passivity on the other? When does healthy reflection become cowardly vacillation? These questions are crucial for our whole society, and the answers to them will determine our future.

My interest at this moment, however, is in how these questions relate to faith. Specifically, how can I honestly commit myself to God and His purposes in the day to day reality of human life without denying the complexity, uncertainty, and diversity that my experiences and reflection suggest to me? If there is an excess of rigid, intolerant "true believers," there is also no shortage of anxious handwringers, and I wish to be neither. For all my own circuitous route through faith, I find my compassion for spiritual wanderers mixed with weariness regarding those who make a fetish of their struggle, who nurse their little doubts like a sick puppy, never genuinely seeking relief or direction, preferring to make the cultivation of doubts itself a way of life.

In filling up these pages with tepid assertions, qualifications, and qualifications of my qualifications, I occasionally think of Russian, Chinese, Central American, or inner-city Christians and am threatened with self-contempt. Do they sit around manipulating thoughts about the psychology of belief and disbelief or the relationship between faith and reason or the tough life of the poor, abused reflective Christian? Not likely. Their circumstances simplify many things. They have experienced evil in its more naked forms. They see more clearly the results of a view of life that ignores the transcendent. Having neither the leisure nor the inclination for going through intellectual permutations with the faith that alone sustains them, theirs is a kind of commitment worth study and emulation.

But I am not a Russian or Chinese Christian. I am not even like many believers I know who find faith a serenely natural and unquestionable response to God. I must work, as God must, with what I am—the product of many forces and unique experiences—and I must find my way, however idiosyncratic or self-indulgent that may seem to others.

And that way, the best that I can tell, is the way of commitment, the way of risk, the way of accepting and utilizing my humanity to serve God who created me and all things. People find and hold on to God in a limitless number of ways, and I have no desire to make mine the paradigm. I could not even fully explain how and why I hold the faith that I do. There are certain things, however, that in my personal synthesis of faith make commitment possible for me. Three of these are *the use of memory, the experience of community,* and *the exercise of perseverance.*

MEMORY

Without memory, human life is not possible in the way we know it. Only by remembering are we able to achieve any thickness to our lives. I learned recently of a man who, because of a World War II trauma, has only a five-minute memory for anything occurring to him since that time. He is constantly reinventing reality. Every face he meets is a new face, even of those who care for him daily; every experience is a new experience. It is difficult to imagine a worse fate, continually cut off from one's own experience, retaining nothing, building on nothing, relating to nothing.

The investigation of memory has been one of the major intellectual and artistic endeavors in modern times. Not only Freud, Jung, and the depth psychologists, but also philosophers, novelists, poets, and painters have underscored the importance of our memory of the past, conscious or unconscious, in shaping our present and future. The French philosopher Henri Bergson, for instance, recognized (as did James Joyce, Virginia Woolf, and other modernist writers) that the past is never really past:

> In reality, the past is preserved by itself, automatically. In its entirety, probably, it follows us at every instant; all that we have felt, thought and willed from our earliest infancy is there, leaning over the present which is about to join it, pressing against the portals of consciousness that would fain leave it outside. . . . Doubtless we think with only a small part of our past, but it is with our entire past, including the original bent of our soul, that we desire, will and act.[1]

Conscious and unconscious memory helps determine both our personal and our corporate lives. We are, in part, the memories of what we have been as individuals, and as joined together with others. In accepting the Nobel Prize, Alexander Solzhenitsyn meditated on the tragic results of the loss of collective memory: "But woe to the nation whose literature is cut off by the interposition of force. That is not simply a violation of 'freedom of the press'; it is stopping up the nation's heart, carving out the nation's memory. The nation loses its memory; it loses its spiritual unity—and, despite their supposedly common language, fellow countrymen suddenly cease understanding each other." [2]

In the same way, memory is crucial to the life of faith. Without memory the church cannot exist, and neither can an individual believer. The Scriptures repeat time and again the importance of remembering. Abraham is sustained by his memory of the promise. The Israelites are constantly admonished to remember their special status before God, particularly as demonstrated by the many things God has done for His people. They are not encouraged to remember abstract concepts about God, but to recall His specific acts. Lapses of memory are at the heart of Israel's problems in the Old Testament. The prophets act as the memory of the people, reminding them of the crucial link between the past and the future, between memory and prophecy. Faith derives from a relationship, not a set of beliefs, and the proper use of memory reminds that God has been trustworthy.

Memory is no less important for the Christian than for the Jew. The Gospels preserve the memory of the life and resurrection of Christ. The writers of the Epistles call on Christians to remember what has been taught them and appeal to the memory of their own direct experience with Christ (e.g., the opening verses of 1 John). Perhaps the most eloquent testimony to the importance of memory is chapter 11 of Hebrews, a passage of Scripture cherished for its celebration of faith, but which is as much about memory, without which faith is not possible.

We are called in these verses to remember the great men and women of faith, people whose lives offer evidence that faith in God is not mere wishing. From Abel to Noah to Abraham to Moses to Gideon and beyond we find as a common denominator to their lives that they believed God when external circumstances dictated that such belief was foolishness. Noah responded to "things not yet seen," Abraham began a journey "not knowing where he was going," Moses renounced the rewards of privilege and "By faith he left Egypt, not fearing the wrath of the king; for he endured, as seeing Him who is unseen." And for each one whose name has been recorded there are countless known only to God, those who "were tortured, not accepting their release, in order that they might obtain a better resurrection; and others experienced mockings and scourgings, yes, also chains and imprisonment."

Passages like this are as important as anything in Scripture to my desire to be a part of the body of believers. Were I to view them from outside faith, I doubt they would move me at all. But I do not look from outside, nor do I believe such a view would be more accurate than my own. I was born into a family of believers, in a line of believers, in a culture where Christian belief has been central. I am no longer bothered, as I once was, by the notion that if I were born in another place or at another time I would have been a Buddhist, or atheist, or animist. I was not born in another place or time, and I am accountable only for my response to what has been presented to me in the uniqueness of my life.

And part of what has been presented to me is a history of faithfulness, a long lineage of men and women of all places and times and ages and races and classes stretching back to creation who have founded their lives on the reasonable expectation that God exists and cares for His creation. And for this faith many "were stoned, they were sawn in two, . . . they were put to death with the sword; they went about in sheepskins, in goatskins, being destitute, afflicted, ill-treated ([people] of whom the world was not worthy), wandering in deserts and mountains and caves and holes in the ground."

How am I to relate to such a history, to such a hope? How much power should I grant my doubts and "objections" to this faith for which these people gave everything? Did I invent doubting? Have I seen more clearly than these the problems of belief? Am I more sensitive to the heartbreaking dilemma of evil and suffering? Does my sophistication expose their childish naiveté? Has my century, the age of killing without parallel, learned so much that now, alas, I must see them as primitives and illusion followers? Has true wisdom come so late to humankind?

I think not. I will remember Abel, who was counted righteous, and who, "through faith, though he is dead, . . . still speaks." I will remember Enoch, whose life demonstrated that "he who comes to God must believe that He is, and that He is a rewarder of those who seek Him." I will remember Abraham, who "was looking for the city which has foundations, whose architect and builder is God." I will remember Sarah, and Joseph, and David, and Samuel, and all those nameless women and men who called caves their home and of whom the world and I are not in the least worthy.

And when faith is too hard, when calculating reason is too insistent, when the contempt of the world (whether within the church or without) is too bitter to bear, then I will call to memory those who were stoned, sawn in two, and made destitute for the sake of faith. Then my burden will be shamefully light, even laughable, and my knees will be strengthened.

And I am comforted in knowing that the people of faith include Rahab, a whore; David, an adulterer; Peter, a man who lacked self-control; and Paul, seemingly a contentious man, because this reminds me that they were human beings, that they struggled, that they sometimes failed—which is to say that they were something like me.

But my memory, thank God, does not have to stop with biblical examples. I also choose to believe, in part, because of Augustine, who burned with many lusts and yet found God; because of Pascal, who pursued God with all the intensity and honesty of a great mind; because of Milton, another contentious man, whose blind eyes could not prevent the light of God from blazing in his mind and imagination; because of Dostoevsky and Tolstoy; because of Eliot and Bonhoeffer and Solzhenitsyn; and because of unnamed and unknown Christians around the world who at this moment carry on the torch of faith in ways little different from their oppressed biblical counterparts.

And I know, of course, that for every Pascal there is a Voltaire, perhaps a dozen, that for every Kierkegaard there is a Nietzsche, for every Flannery O'Connor or Simone Weil a Virginia Woolf or Ayn Rand. For many of these I have respect—more for a Samuel Beckett who one senses knows something of what he cannot accept, less for a Bertrand Russell who is so clearly ignorant of that which he caricatures.

These people present their own powerful views of the world for our inspection. If you decide that any one or combination of them is the conviction on which you will risk a life, then arguments will not likely convince you otherwise. I can only witness to my own choice, and that is the God of Abraham, of Luke the physician, and of Mother Teresa the bringer of comfort—as manifested in God's Son, Jesus Christ.

My memory includes also the church's memory. It includes its history and traditions, its saints and martyrs, its liturgies and confessions, its mistakes and triumphs. It includes the times when the church has stayed close to God and been true to its own best memory, and also when it has played the world's game of power, prestige, success and has been an instrument of oppression. The church must remember well if it is to function well today. It cannot afford to participate in the mass historical ignorance of our shallow society, much less glory in that ignorance as do some who feel they are the first to discover God's will for His world.

I do not, however, participate only in a corporate memory. I also exercise the memory of my personal encounters with God. (*Personal encounter with God*—what phrase could be more indicative of delusion to the secularized mind?) How can one talk about such things? They do not translate well into words. They are not the hard bullets with which apologetic battles are won. They convince no one not already inclined to belief. One wonders, in retrospect, what they really were, and what is to be made of them. They were sometimes primarily emotional experiences, and emotions fade, and even the memory of them.

What can one claim for a twilight experience on a snowy hillside where one had an infusing sense of the goodness of God? How does one convey the shock of recognition that a demanding prayer one day for God to show Himself had actually been answered in the most concrete way by a letter from a friend *the day before?* What about that childhood walk down the center aisle of a small Baptist church in the Texas panhandle? What of the sense of God's presence in time of crisis, of protection in time of danger, of comfort in time of suffering?

All can be explained away to be sure; all can be rationalized, psychologized, and sanitized. But the secularist explanations pale, especially as I see the shaky ground from which they are launched. Why not simply recall these experiences as moments when the transcendent world intersected my transient one? Why not risk belief instead of unbelief? Both are risks and neither yields to the test tube.

So I call to mind my personal encounters with God, and I name the names of men and women from my own life through whom God has chosen to show Himself if only I choose to see. And I add these to the church's longer memory, and, in short, I believe. This is not mere nostalgia or a sentimental yearning for "the good old days" of simple faith. Neither is it the debilitating practice of feeding parasitically on past experiences (other's or one's own) for lack of present spiritual sustenance.

Instead, memory of the past should energize the present. One does not catalogue memories of God's work or personal experiences like artifacts in a museum. Rather, the past animates and is made new in the present. The museum mentality of static preservation, so common in the church, gives way to anticipation and expectation of a new work in a new time by the ever-creative spirit of God working, as always, through His people.

The writer of Hebrews is not content simply to list the great men and women of faith, known and unknown; at the beginning of Chapter 12, he draws a practical conclusion: "Therefore, since we have so great a cloud of witnesses surrounding us, let us also lay aside every encumbrance, and the sin which so easily entangles us, and let us run with endurance the race that is set before us, fixing our eyes on Jesus, the author and perfecter of faith. . . ." This image of "a cloud of witnesses" is both inspiring and sobering. The believer is part of a tradition that stretches back to creation. Each of us has the choice whether to make our contribution to that tradition, to our collective memories, or to reject it. The Abrahams and Rahabs and Gideons and nameless martyrs have made their choice. The Augustines and Pascals and Solzhenitsyns and unknown oppressed believers have made theirs as well. And we, with no more or less risk than they, will make ours.

There is a shorthand name we give to all our memories— *tradition*. It is a term to which people respond in very divergent ways, but in matters of faith, it is only valuable when it is internalized and made individual. It becomes *my* tradition, which I know and value, which has its own unique shape because I and my life are unique. The Christian tradition will be slightly different because I choose to be part of it. It is not something I relate to objectively because neither I nor it are objects. Tradition is not primarily a set of creeds or theologies, though these are included, but a history of persons and communities and relationships. And when I see faith in terms of the struggle of people, alone and together, to know and be known by God, then I do not object to the risk that is the price for being part of that struggle.

COMMUNITY

Creating a pantheon of spiritual heroes is easily done, perhaps because I do not have to actually live with any of these people in their full humanity. Barnabas might have been slower to canonize the apostle Paul than were subsequent Christians because he had to live with him—no easy task. (He would also, however, have been much slower to dismiss Paul's view of some things which many contemporary Christians and secularists find offensive to their modern sensibilities.) Living in community with Christians can be simultaneously a foundation for faith and a sore trial of that faith.

The reflective Christian often feels great ambivalence about his or her experience as part of a specific community of believers. There is something wonderfully attractive about the metaphor of the church as a body—mutually supportive, each part performing a unique function for the good of all, each making possible and delighting in the others' success.

At the same time, there is something repellent about the distortions of community as actually practiced so often in the church. The pressure for uniformity, the spirit of legalism, the use of Christianity to sanctify cultural fetishes, and a host of other problems common in the church make wholehearted participation difficult for anyone with a sense of self or low tolerance for cliché and hypocrisy.

The supernatural potential of Christians laboring to establish the kingdom of God together is so great that the reality of life in the typical church is both depressing and comic by comparison. The church is easily ridiculed and, in its institutional form, deserves much of the abuse it receives. What is amazing, however, is not that the church suffers from every kind of failing common to human beings, but that simultaneously it is still the primary instrument of God's work on earth.

Flannery O'Connor recognized this paradox in one of her letters: "I think that the Church is the only thing that is going to make the terrible world we are coming to endurable; the only thing that makes the Church endurable is that it is somehow the body of Christ and that on this we are fed." [3] Who would not reject the church if it were not for this "somehow"? What person of integrity would put up with the weakness of the church if it were not that God still called us together? And what are those weaknesses but our own, which we do not leave behind when we abandon the church, leaving instead only those redeeming strengths that come from sharing lives together?

Life shared in community is a powerfully attractive concept but, like that of tradition, becomes personally life-shaping only when abstractions give way to persons. I would not risk any more to preserve the church as an institution and organization than I would to save the Eiffel Tower or the Taj Mahal, probably less. But to have a part in the genuine work of God in the world together with others whom I love and respect is worth any risk that I can imagine. It infuses my life with a sense of meaning and solidarity that I find nowhere else.

This is not faith in God, the secularist might respond, but merely the human desire for the security of the group. Perhaps so, but why not? Some people seek this security and sense of purpose in politics, or social organizations, or in money, or in rooting for the local football team. That I find it, in part, in identifying with others who, like Pascal, have not been able to attach themselves wholly to the things of this world is neither evidence for nor against faith. It is, however, an important and valid ingredient in my personal decision to take the risk that faith requires.

That risk would not be justified if, like many, I focused on human failure. The dozen hypocrites I see sitting around me, the trio of gossips sharing the same pew, the wearying legalist sitting on the platform, do not interest me nearly so much (are not their banal sins merely my own?) as that quiet one with the gift of prayer, or that other one with a hunger for righteousness. A painter seeks inspiration from the work of the few masters and is not distracted by the infinite number of bad paintings by those with little talent or dedication. My ultimate model, of course, is Christ, but I draw strength and daring from seeing His image reflected in the lives of even a few of my fellow believers.

It is not my purpose to enumerate the many benefits of intertwining one's life with other believers. There are many good books, ancient and modern, on Christian community. I would like to mention two benefits, however, that are particularly significant for the reflective Christian. One involves the testing of faith. Robert McAfee Brown points out the value of testing one's individual faith against the larger and longer experience of the community, thereby guarding against narrowness and mere idiosyncrasy.[4] The corporate preservation of truth from the danger of unchecked individualism is a traditional and valuable function of the church.

At the same time, however, the community can also test *its* faith, as Brown suggests, against the faith of the individual.

At times the larger body of believers should weigh itself in
light of the example of the minority. How rarely this is done.
How reluctant the protectors of the status quo are to see the
value of the fresh expression, the creative application, the revi-
talizing animation that keeps God's truth from ossifying in
our timid hands.

Brown points out a second benefit of community that is
largely ignored but of potentially great importance for the
reflective Christian. The community is "the place where the
burden of doubt can be shared." [5] This idea is so appropriate
for a community of believers yet so foreign to actual practice.
We are to be, as Brown points out, burden bearers for one
another, and doubt is one of those burdens. As a member of
a fellowship of believers, I do not have to hold together the
whole complex of Christian faith and practice by myself. I
do not have to do everything that the whole body of Christ
should do or be everything it should be. In a sense, I do not
even have to believe without ever faltering everything the body
of Christ should believe.

This concept can obviously be abused, but it has merit. Sometimes life's troubles may so overwhelm me that I cannot for
a time sustain a belief in God's loving concern for me and
my fellow creatures. In my humanity I may, like many of
my biblical predecessors in the faith, despair or even rage
against God. At that point you must believe for me. Do not
insist that I still believe. Do not whip the mule that has col-
lapsed under the burden. Do what you can to lighten the burden
and wait patiently until I have regained my strength. And
someday I will do the same for you.

There are biblical precedents for this. Henri Nouwen refers
to one in a journal entry from his time in a Trappist monastery:

Today: feast of St. Thomas the Apostle. During a dialogue
homily, two of the monks remarked in different ways that although
Thomas did not believe in the resurrection of the Lord, he kept
faithful to the community of the apostles. In that community the
Lord appeared to him and strengthened his faith. I find this a

very profound and consoling thought. In times of doubt or unbelief, the community can "carry you along," so to speak; it can even offer on your behalf what you yourself overlook, and can be the context in which you may recognize the Lord again.[6]

The community of believers is the "context" within which most of us will "recognize the Lord." Few things are as desirable as being part of such a community when it is working as God designed it. Even when it is something less, however, the Christian cannot escape the corporateness of faith. We did not ourselves inaugurate faith in God, and we do well to maximize the benefits that derive from shared commitment.

The hopelessly shallow contemporary mind sees in community the loss of freedom. Karl Barth, on the other hand, expresses beautifully the greater truth that life together is itself a wise expression of individual freedom:

Each individual is called to this commitment in the midst of the community of men, not as the first disciple but as a follower in the visible and invisible footsteps of many; not as the only one but together with many known and unknown fellow Christians. He may be accompanied by the comforting help of several or by at least a few. He may be a rather sad member of the rear guard. or he may be way ahead of the crowd where he is temporarily alone. He lives for himself, but not only for himself. He is constantly in living relationship to others, as a member of the people of God who appropriates for himself God's election and is responsible for the brothers.[7]

Just as we are chosen by and choose God, so we choose and are chosen in uniting our lives with fellow believers. We share the joy, we share the doubt, we share the risk. We also share our warts and weaknesses. Paul longed to be with the believers in Rome so "that I may be encouraged together with you while among you, each of us by the other's faith, both yours and mine" (Rom. 1:12). I know very well how short the church falls in living up to its high calling, but I have also tasted enough of the supernatural power that is available

to Christians working out their salvations together to know
that somewhere about here God is to be found.

PERSEVERANCE

Nothing worthwhile is easy, certainly not the life of faith
in the twentieth century. Faith can be simultaneously incredi-
bly strong and painfully fragile. Doctrines of eternal security
notwithstanding, the choice to discontinue the whole experiment of seeking God is always present—as is the choice to
begin, or to begin once more. These choices are sometimes
made consciously, often by default. We tire of the struggle
of faith as an athlete tires in a contest or a soldier grows
weary in battle.

This awareness has brought the concept of perseverance near
the center of my own choice to continue the often difficult
dialogue with God. Perseverance means carrying on in the
face of obstacles, continuing in what one is doing despite unfa-
vorable circumstances. The marathoner perseveres despite a
protesting body, the sculptor perseveres despite the unyielding
stone, the husband and wife persevere despite the strains of
marriage.

In the things of the spirit, perseverance means continuing
in faith when the conditions for faith are unpropitious. The
Bible is a very realistic book. Its writers understand human
psychology and the realities of life far better than most modern
practitioners of mental therapy. It is full of encouragement
to take heart in the midst of struggle, and of admonitions
that the long run is more important than the short. The writer
of Hebrews, as we have seen, exhorts us to "run *with endurance*
the race that is set before us" (12:1, emphasis mine), and assures
us we are "partakers of Christ, *if we hold fast* the beginning
of our assurance firm *until the end*" (3:14, emphasis mine).
Paul encourages us to "not lose heart in doing good, for in
due time we shall reap *if we do not grow weary*" (Gal. 6:9,
emphasis mine). Christ Himself tells the disciples, "You will

be hated by all on account of My name, but it is the one who has *endured to the end* who will be saved" (Matt. 10:22, emphasis mine).

The Bible promises difficulty, suffering, even hatred for those who persist in faith. Who needs it? Why put yourself through that kind of hassle? Life is too short. Why not accommodate oneself to the world's values and keep low—especially when one cannot be sure that Christianity is true anyway? One answer, among many, is that difficulty, suffering, and hatred are part of the nature of human life and you'll get your share no matter what you choose. The book of Job speaks for believers and nonbelievers alike when it says, "man is born for trouble,/As sparks fly upward" (5:7). We do not choose between a life of difficulty and a life of ease. We simply choose *for what purpose* we will work, sometimes suffer, and hopefully endure. I may have more pain than my secular neighbor; I may have less. In either case, my struggles are given an ultimate meaning by the context of a life lived in light of eternity.

Significantly, the pessimistic words in Job about the inevitability of trouble are followed with an affirmation (5:8–9):

> "But as for me, I would seek God.
> And I would place my cause before God;
> Who does great and unsearchable things,
> Wonders without number."

These are my words as well. I am keenly aware that humankind is born to trouble. It is painfully clear to me that I do not have absolute certainty that anything I believe is true. My reason is inadequate in these things to guide me to a sure conclusion; my emotions often fail me (not infrequently by their absence). But I will remember that others have endured this situation before me. I will call to mind their testimony and my own of encounters with God. *Memory.* I will seek out the fellowship of others who likewise struggle. I will forgive them their trespasses as they forgive me mine. *Community.* I will seek to run the race with endurance, to fare foreward when forces without and within counsel abandonment. *Perseverance.*

*   *   *   *   *

Alex's strongest desire was for the oblivion of sleep. The conference had not refreshed him as he had hoped. The weight of his own mediocrity oppressed his spirit. His blood felt thick and tepid in his veins. Longing vaguely for a different life, he went to bed in a mood not conducive to pleasant dreams. . . .

The guard opened the door to the cell almost politely and stood aside for me to pass, as though into his drawing room for an after dinner smoke. My eyes had still not adjusted from the walk across the bright prison yard. I found the bunk by knocking into it as I shuffled forward. There was no outside window, and the small rectangular grill in the door diffused the weak light of a naked bulb well down the corridor.

I sat on the bunk, my back against the cold stone block wall, my feet on the floor, staring into the darkness. From that darkness materialized, so slowly that I was only slightly startled, a face. The forehead came first, then the nose and cheeks, petal pale against the dark, so dark it seemed to make a sound. I could see no eyes, only two more circles of black echoing the greater black all around. Where there should have been a jaw or mouth, I perceived a beard, reddish at the roots even in the dark, but merging into the blackness so that it had no apparent end.

I did not speak at first. There was only the slightest evidence that anything was there. The face, if there at all, was only six feet away; it could as well have been in another galaxy. It betrayed no motion, merely suspended, a minor moon of a minor planet, far removed from its minor sun.

Even in its tenuousness, the face conveyed a powerful mixture of great sadness and strength. For a moment I thought of Captain Ahab and felt myself a forlorn Ishmael.

Speech, I thought, might blow this apparition away. To simply stare at it was unnerving.

"My name is Alex."

There was no answer. My voice sounded weak and childish to me. Now I was frightened. This gauze spirit must either speak or go away.

"Do you have a name? Do you speak English? Please say something."

I heard a sigh on the air. From the darkness of the beard came a voice as old and slow and strong as the stones in the walls of the cell.

"You will learn, comrade, that one does not speak to just anyone. Speech is rationed here, like everything else."

I did not feel this an encouragement to further conversation, but I feared silence more than scorn.

"I don't know where I am or why I'm here. I can't remember what led up to this, and I don't know what is going to happen. Can you help me?"

There was no response. My speaking seemed to have thickened the darkness, or taken strength from my eyes, for I was no longer sure I could see the face. Long moments passed, and then the voice again.

"Where are you? You are in prison. Why are you here? Because it was appointed so, by mutual consent of the powers that be. How did it happen? It does not matter. What is going to happen? That is up to you. Can I help you? Probably not."

I did not like this riddling response. It portended secret knowledge. This fellow, evidently, was going to play the cryptic at my expense. And yet, I could not help but feel he was my only salvation, and I wanted more than anything that he simply keep speaking.

"Could I ask your name?"

"Our names, apparently, are the same. I am Alexander Isaevich. Next, you will want to know why I am in prison. Yes? It is a natural question for an outsider to ask, but you will learn not to ask it. People are here for every reason and for no reason. Eventually you will find out who has been accused of what, but it is not information you should seek. Someone may cut your throat for asking and that will be the answer to your question."

He stopped as though from tiredness, and then continued. "But I will tell you myself why I am here. I have not told many. My general crime, it could be said, is thinking myself a human being. I have acted as though being human included certain responsibilities. I have arrogantly respected myself. I have decided there are some things I will not do."

He paused and I felt he was reliving in his mind something from his past.

"My specific crime is to believe that I did not make myself. It is finding something larger than myself and our collective selves. That belief itself was not my real crime, however. It was acting as though it were true. Yes, the acting is the crime. They don't really care what you think. Behavior is all. I simply misbehaved."

"What do you mean? Did you go to church, or pray before a meal or something?"

The darkness below his nose opened up as he laughed, the light reflecting faintly off his teeth.

"No, no. I rarely went to church. They would not throw me in prison for that. My church has the seal of approval. And I have not prayed before a meal since I was a child. These are forms that I do not keep myself. But, as I think of it, it was as a young child that my troubles with the authorities began. I must have been about ten years old. We were studying science in school and visiting the class that day was a well-known astronomer in our region. They never missed a chance to mock religious belief in those days, even more so than now perhaps. I remember my teacher asking him during his talk if his studies had taught him anything about the existence of God. It was clearly a planted question. 'I have been looking through telescopes for thirty years,' he said, 'and I haven't seen a single angel. Nor any trace of a heaven.'

"Well I burst out laughing at this, and soon all the other children were laughing too. The teacher smiled because she thought their little ploy had worked well. 'Aren't people foolish to believe in angels and heaven, Alexander?' she asked to reinforce the point. 'I don't know, madam,' I responded. 'I was laughing at how stupid it is to think a telescope would help you find out one way or the other.'

"I was severely punished for that remark you can be sure, but I have been laughing at them ever since—not always merrily, but laughing nonetheless. As I grew older, my laughter took different forms, as did their punishments. And here I am."

He lapsed into silence. I had made peace with the dark so that now I could see his full head and figure. His eyes were closed and he sat Buddha-like for many minutes. I yearned for him to speak again.

"Have you been in prison long?" I asked.

I thought perhaps he smiled slightly.

"Long? Have I been in prison long? Perhaps the better question would be, 'Was there ever a time I wasn't in prison?' I don't think that would be too cynical to ask. But you are thinking in terms of months and years behind walls and wire. Let me see. I was in the first time for three years. Just a taste you might say, an appetizer. The next time for five, theoretically, though it somehow became seven. After that for different periods in different places.

"It really is the places more than the time that make an impression. Yes, I have spent much of my time in the wastelands, in the bitter places, so cold and forsaken the guards felt they also were being punished, as, in fact, they were . . . but with no redemption for their suffering. No, with no redemption for them. And shall I tell you what I learned there? Shall I tell you, a young man, a very ancient and simple truth it took me years of imprisonment to learn? It is so obvious it makes me laugh to think how few understand it these days. It's simply this: there is good and there is evil, and the difference between them is absolute.

"If you do not believe this, it is because you have eaten too well for too long. You have read books at your ease written by others at their ease. If you stay here long, and who ever just visits, these illusions will drop from your eyes. Evil will become more real to you than your own face or that of your beloved, both of which will fade quickly. Evil will be your instructor, your companion, your terror. And good, when you find it, often in the unexpected places, will seem the most precious of things. It will be redeemed for you from the clutches of the insipid priest, the humanitarian, the do-gooder, the liberal politician, the teacher of ethics. Good will become for you the force behind the world—now in ascendency, now in eclipse—which hates evil and struggles to destroy it. And you will want, if you can stay human, to be on the side of that good more than you care for your own life."

He repeated as though to himself, "if you can stay human . . . if you can stay human." And then, in a whisper, "That is not easy, God knows."

As I sat in the darkness and the silence, a fear grew up that this man would be taken from me. Nothing seemed important but that I stay near and listen to him speak. I had the irrational dread that the guard would come back and tell me I was released and that I had to return to the streets. As much to quell this rising panic as anything else, I asked another question.

"Has it really been worth it to have suffered so much for something so, well, so fragile as faith in God? I mean, couldn't you have been a believer without letting it get you in so much trouble? If that's too personal, you know, you don't have to answer it. Just sort of thinking out loud."

I was afraid I had spoken out of turn, that I had raised an embarrassing question which I wanted to retract. He waved away my sputtering with an uplifted hand.

"No, no. Do not apologize. It is the only important question you have asked. And since we may have very little time together, it is good. . . . Is it worth it all? Is it worth it all? Haven't I asked myself that question ten thousand times? Haven't I given every possible answer to it?

"To answer it now, I suppose, I must go back four hundred years when my ancestors came to this land from the south and east. They came as wanderers and found a place to call their own. They also found a faith. They became Christians here. All of them, most on the same day. You may say they merely traded one religion for another. I do not see it that way. Christianity was a richer soil, like the soil for farming they found, not because they merely felt it was richer, but because it was. From this day on, said the patriarch of my ancestors, we will follow the ways of the Christ. And so they did, and so did their children, and their children's children until the times when we can put names with those who went before us and can tell their story in detail.

"And some became priests and others soldiers, but most were farmers and laborers and craftsmen. Some were devout and others were not, but all continued to say, 'I and mine are followers of the Christ.' And my family gave more than they could afford of labor and money to build the churches, and they gave their sons to serve in them, and more than a few, God rest their souls, gave their lives, in this century and before, rather than break the ancient pledge.

"And I? What have I learned in my life that should make it different for me? What book or teacher has been so persuasive that I would renounce my part? What doubt so powerful that all who went before are tossed aside? Do I not have my doubts? They are ferocious. Have I not reasons for disbelief? My experiences are crushing. Could I not believe in safer ways? I have longed for a quiet, comfortable life.

"But then I think of that ten-year-old boy who laughed at their foolishness and was right to laugh. God preserve in me the simplicity that brought that laughter to my lips. And I see before me my ancestors over the years, asking anxiously, 'What is it, Alexander Isaevich? What is it you have learned that we didn't know? What richer soil have you found? Were we wrong to have followed the Christ? Is there now, in your time, a better way? Tell us, so that we may know and weep for our foolishness.'

"And I must say to them with all my heart, 'No. No. You were right to follow the Christ. I also follow. There has been found no better way. Now, as then, there are many illusions. Rest, beloved ancestors, you did well. I come soon to be with you.' "

He put his head in his hands and said no more. The sound

of a turning key in the door froze my heart. The guard stood in the open doorway and looked at me. "It's 6:30, you sleepy head. Time to get up and hit the freeway. Don't want to keep the boss waiting, ha, ha. And while you're shaving make sure you stay tuned to 'Real Radio' KXOX, where the weather may be cold but the music is HOT. Brought to you this morning by Benny's. . . ."

Alex silenced the radio with a hand. Pulling the blankets over his head, he mourned with a painful heart the thinness of his life.

*   *   *   *   *

Flannery O'Connor's mother had a name for any milk cow on their farm which did not produce milk. She called it "a boarder," [8] that is, one which accepts its keep without giving anything in return. Every cause and every society has its boarders as well, and Christianity has more than its share. Reflective Christians are particularly susceptible to this condition because of their difficulty in choosing between competing alternatives.

Perhaps the greatest barrier to commitment in our age is the widespread sense that truth and goodness, if they exist at all, are so fragmented, so mixed together with error and evil, so easily perverted, so scattered amongst all competing causes, that to choose one cause, one way of seeing things, is to do violence to truth and goodness rather than to serve them. Even as I write these words, they are strangely powerful to me. "Yes," I tell myself, obedient to the secular orthodoxy in which I have been bathed, "who am I to say what is right and wrong? How do I have the presumption to say this is the direction in which truth lies, that is the way of falsehood and illusion?"

I have the presumption because, essentially, I have no choice but to choose. Not to choose is, itself, to make a choice, one no less presumptuous than any other. Kierkegaard saw that refusing to choose simply meant allowing others to choose for you. Choices cannot be avoided. Sartre grasps part of this truth when he says we are *condemned* to be free. Because we are free moral agents whose lives are shaped by the pattern of our choices, we cannot escape the sometimes crushing responsibility of choice and action. Pretending we will only choose when the correct choice is clear, thereby lessening our chances of choosing wrongly, soils us with one of the most damning errors of all—moral passivity in a world desperate for moral courage.

Pascal saw clearly the essential cowardice of those who hide behind relativism to excuse their unwillingness to pursue and affirm truth: "Those who do not love the truth take as a pretext that it is disputed, and that a multitude deny it." [9] We can see the human desire for certainty and inviolable security for what it is—an understandable but ultimately doomed rebellion against human finitude. And yet, the reflective Christian must resist the erroneous conclusion that commitment is therefore impossible or unjustified.

Not only should we risk commitment despite uncertainty, I would argue we must choose commitment precisely because of uncertainty. The precariousness of life is all the more reason to risk acting in faith. Life is no less risky for the secularist; the ultimate goal is simply much less. Pascal saw faith as an intelligent wager. The secularist is also wagering, only with far more disastrous consequences if wrong.

Faith, however, is not a matter of rolling the dice. It is, or can be, a conscious expression of a great gift—human freedom. God has given us all the ability to either choose or reject a relationship with Him. Without this freedom, commitment would be inconceivable, since the concept only has meaning when there is the possibility of doing otherwise. Barth says freedom rightly understood is not primarily freedom *from* something, the popular notion springing from the desire to shed responsibility, "but freedom *to* and *for*," a release to choice and action.[10] And the greatest exercise of that freedom, Kierkegaard affirms, is to choose God, to choose commitment and responsibility, to acknowledge individually and in community with others the obedience to God which an appropriate use of freedom suggests.

Through commitment, truth becomes a lived reality rather

than an abstraction. As it resides in a set of creeds, or a code
of ethics, or a political or philosophical manifesto, or even a
passage of Scripture, truth is a kind of potential energy, latent
but unrealized. Only as it is manifested in the particularity
of my life, giving shape to my relationships, thoughts, and
acts, does truth become more than the battered plaything of
competing world views.

The embodiment of truth through the free choice of commitment is the only hope of a troubled world. Commitment is
the cure for the sophomoric cynicism which thinks it has had
the last word when it smugly asks, "What *is* truth?" Flannery
O'Connor rightly observed, "If you live today you breathe
in nihilism. In or out of the Church, it's the gas you breathe." [11]
Cynicism is the spiritual manifestation of the nihilistic tenden-
cies in much of modern thought, and reflective people are
especially susceptible to it.

Cynicism may seem an intelligent position, given the hypocrisy and stupidity of many human endeavors. Cynics often
pride themselves on their greater insight into human nature
and society, fancying that they see through sham and preten-
sions that fool everyone else. Ultimately, however, cynicism
is both foolish and cowardly itself. It is foolish because it underestimates the God-given human potential for finding and creating meaning in life, and it is cowardly because it is afraid to
risk anything in the human adventure. The cynical spirit, like
many others, insists on certainty before it will affirm and, lack-
ing that, retreats into the false security of denial and hum-
bugging.

Helmut Thielicke points out that nihilism, crippling relativism, and cynicism result from approaching life as a spectator.
The spectator is detached, supposedly objective, uninvolved.
This is a false, even inhuman, relationship to life. It turns
people into objects and makes values arbitrary and statistical.
Commitment removes one from the spectator role, and "one
is set free from nihilistic despair the moment one is confronted
with a genuine human task, however small it may be. . . ." [12]

As Christians in the late twentieth century, we have specific historical tasks to accomplish (one of which is to offer a credible alternative to the nihilistic spirit of our age), and it is *in the doing of these tasks* that faith will be verified and the force of doubts lessened. When one attempts a life of commitment, doubt and theoretical questions do not disappear, but they become surprisingly less central. Things that once loomed large diminish in point and relevance as one gets on with the business of trying to live a life under God.

Given the nature of our world, personal neutrality is evil. It makes more possible Auschwitz, the hungry and abused child, the devaluation of human life, the oppression of the weak by the strong. T. S. Eliot is right to prefer the blasphemer who struggles against God to the passive modern man and woman who are indifferent to all things spiritual.[13] The antidote to neutrality, as to cynicism, is commitment, and the key to commitment is the exercise of the will.

The human will—so powerful, so tenacious, so weak, so easily paralyzed. Reflective people especially often suffer from overdeveloped analytic abilities and underdeveloped wills. Kierkegaard observed that "a habit of vacillation is the absolute ruin of every spiritual relationship"[14] and that it is "not so much a question of choosing between willing the good *or* the evil, as of choosing to *will* . . ."[15] at all.

Exercising the will is difficult because it involves our fear of risk and the unknown. Even if one's present life seems unsatisfactory, one can identify with the old saying, "the devil you know is better than the devil you don't know." We prolong the certain pain in the tooth rather than face the uncertain pain in the dentist's office.

And yet risk, as we have seen, is indispensable to any significant life, nowhere more clearly than in the life of the spirit. The goal of faith is not to create a set of immutable, rationalized, precisely defined and defendable beliefs to preserve forever. It is to recover a relationship with God. He offers us a person and a relationship; we want rules and a format. He offers us security through risk; we want safety through certainty. He offers us unity and community; we want unanimity and institutions. And it does no good to point fingers because none of us desires too much light. All of us want God to behave Himself in our lives, to touch this area but leave that one alone, to empower us here but let us run things ourselves over there.

Faith in God, then, is not a belief system to defend but a life to live out (though systematic thinking about our beliefs can help us decide how to live). Mistaking this active life of faith for an institutionally backed and culturally bound belief system is similar to reducing the *Mona Lisa* to paint-by-numbers. Anyone can see that the paint-by-numbers picture has a relationship to the original, but how foolish to think they are the same thing. This is not at all an argument against the church, whose role I take to be crucial. Rather, it is an argument for the personal, risky, never-completed nature of our relationship to God. My desire is for an open-eyed commitment to the life of faith, and the responsibilities it entails, that includes a sensitivity to the great tensions under which faith must live in the modern world.

As a belief system, the Christian religion is subject to the many ills of all belief systems; as an encounter with God, it transforms individual lives and human history. God does not give us primarily a belief system; he gives us Himself, most clearly in the person of Jesus Christ, so that truth and meaning can be ours through a commitment to that love with which He first loved us. The risk is great, but the reward is infinite.

6
Surviving As a Reflective Christian

*The spiritual man differs...in being able
to endure isolation....*
—Kierkegaard

*We are worthy of being believed only as we
[are] aware of our unworthiness.*
—Karl Barth

*Do not be excessively righteous, and do not
be overly wise.*
—Ecclesiastes 7:16

DECIDING TO RISK COMMITMENT is one thing; living that out in the concreteness of daily life is another. How often laudable human intentions break against the rocks of everyday mundane existence. The slow, endless lapping of the waves does more to turn the rocks to sand than the fury of the occasional storm. If I am to persevere to the end in the risky life for God, I need a strategy for survival that guards against both the pressure to wholly conform to the subcultures and the self-delusions of my own heart.

For the most part, I can neither walk away from or live in total harmony with the two subcultures I have described. The place where one first finds God puts a mark on you that is not easily removed, nor should it be. Likewise, once ignited, the fire of the intellect is not easily extinguished, nor should it be either.

Because of this situation, the thoughtful Christian will often be in conflict—sometimes with others, sometimes with him-or herself, sometimes with God. If this conflict is not to destroy or diminish lives, it must be dealt with properly. The goal is not a life of frictionless ease (without friction, nothing in the physical world can move), but to be in right standing before God.

Pascal offers what could be taken as a prayer for those who find themselves in conflict: "Let God, out of His compassion, having no regard to the evil which is in me, and having regard to the good which is in you, grant us all grace that truth may not be overcome in my hands. . . ." [1]

Nothing should be of higher value to the reflective Christian in difficult circumstances than an unqualified desire to see truth triumph. One should wish passionately that it prevail, should love it more than one's own prestige or sense of security. Nothing will set you apart more clearly. The average person, observes Kierkegaard, "lives in the sensuous categories agreeable/

disagreeable"—in terms both of his stomach and his mind—
and does not suspect that "standing in relationship to the truth
. . . [is] the highest good." [2]

The pursuit of truth and the love of God are one and the
same. One does not choose between them, as many in both
subcultures suggest. Simone Weil saw that we can even wrestle
with God, and particularly our distorted notion of God, on
this ground: "It seems certain to me that we can never resist
God enough (!), if we do it from a pure regard for the truth.
Christ loves those who prefer the truth, because before he is
Christ he is the truth. If we turn away from him, however,
to follow truth, we will not go far before walking into his
arms again." [3] This affirmation is not counsel for playing cava-
lierly with one's faith in Christ, and it must be tempered by
the realization that what we take for truth is sometimes illusion,
but it expresses the central role that truth-seeking has in the
life of the reflective believer.

Such truth-seeking is incompatible with arrogance and self-
satisfaction. What can the arrogant man or woman learn? Who
can teach the smug and self-satisfied? Where there is no hunger
or thirst, there is no need for sustenance. We are an age, both
in the church and at large, which does not perceive the value
of brokenness. The aggressive assertion carries the day, the
answerman, the pontificator—even if one is pontificating about
no one having the right to pontificate.

Humility is not synonymous with passivity or indecisiveness.
One can hold beliefs passionately yet with humility. An awareness of the slipperiness of truth, the subtlety of error, and
the human appetite for illusion does not mean one cannot
believe and act with intensity. Acting with less than perfect
knowledge is part of the risk of being human. But we should
therefore reject self-congratulating narrowness, always seeking
a deepening and broadening of our understanding rather than
a hardening of it.

Humility helps us avoid confusing defense of the truth with
defense of the self. This difficult distinction is doubly so for the
typical defender of the faith or the secular intellectual. Self-

defense is so instinctive that neither is likely to seriously question whether his or her cause is truth's cause as well. Barth, on the other hand, cites the Old Testament example of David and Shimei in counseling the church to accept for a moment the criticism of the world in order to see itself honestly and correct its own shortcomings. Individuals and institutions alike need the brokenness of humility if they are to have the teachable spirits necessary to discovering truth.

Humility also helps one recognize that the errors or wickedness of one's "enemies," no matter how grievous, do not ensure one's own correctness or righteousness. How often opposing sides pillory, mock, and caricature the deficiencies of the other as though that alone established their own validity. The preacher eagerly catalogues the disgusting sins of our evil society, oblivious to the beam in his own eye. The vacillating believer points to the hypocrisy and absurdities of the church to implicitly justify his own failure to live an active life of faith. Be honest with yourself and others. If the church is often ridiculous, all the more reason you and I should contribute to its rehabilitation by living correctly before God.

The instinctive reaction to conflict is a combination of self-defense and attack. One ferrets out the errors in an opposing position in a seek-and-destroy mission that supposedly leaves one more secure. The person genuinely committed to truth does better to seek out the kernel of truth that is part of any point of view. Truth is so precious it must be prized wherever it is found. No system of thought, almost no single influential idea, is totally devoid of truth. By ignoring or distorting that truth for the sake of winning arguments, we diminish our own cause.

One must not be naive, however, about the nature of truth. Except at its lowest levels, it does not come as hermetically sealed packets of information or hard nuggets of gold which are the same no matter where they are found. Truth, as we know it at least, exists in a concrete setting in place and time in the midst of human relationships, which greatly effects its nature and function. The abstract statements that we often call "Truth" have their place, but it is as these conceptions take shape in the quotidian world of personal experience that we see them for what they really are. And what we find is that we have the power to release truth or to destroy it depending on the way in which we *use* it.

Truth cannot be adequately evaluated on an objective or propositional level. *How* one holds a truth, one's intention in regard to truth, the use to which a truth is put, the position against which a truth is asserted, the relationship between one truth and an equally valid balancing truth—all these and more determine the ultimate character of truth in our lives. Sadly, even truth can be made to *function* as falsehood when it is fragmented, distorted, or isolated from its position in the whole.

Consider, as an illustration, the relationship of the legalist to God's moral law. When the Pharisee, or his modern Christian counterpart, turns the moral law into a legalistically enforced code for external conduct, the law of God *in that context* loses the force of truth. It may look like God's law, it may sound like God's law, but, because of the spirit in which it is manifested, it is no longer God's law. Similarly, Job's friends spoke many so-called truths to him which taken abstractly are theologically unimpeachable. Scripture recognizes, however, that the cool self-righteousness with which these truths were offered renders them useless to Job or anyone else.

Christ, on the other hand, repeatedly modeled truth as relationship, as part of lived experience. His response to the woman caught in adultery illustrates the higher ground between legalism and license. He rejected the opportunity to make the letter of the law absolute, refusing to treat her as an object against which the law could be exercised. Neither did he sanction adultery as acceptable behavior. Instead, he addressed the woman as an individual person in a very difficult situation. He combined compassion and principle by delivering her from those who would use a moral truth for immoral ends, while reaffirming the validity of God's moral law by telling her to sin no more.

An awareness of the relational nature of truth, together with a vision of truth's wholeness, can help one survive our two subcultures. One is free to affirm truth wherever found, yet wise enough to realize that truth is weakened in certain contexts and can even be made to serve error. At best, it will always, in our finite world, be incomplete. I may learn much about compassion and concern for justice from the secularist, but I see, as he or she does not, that any notion of justice is superficial which ignores its origin in the nature of God. I may affirm with the Christian moralist that homosexuality is wrong, but recognize the immorality of using that truth to question someone's humanity. Reflective Christians should be sensitive to the need for wholeness of truth both in their own lives and in those with whom they are trying to relate.

The complement of an attitude of humility in regard to truth is one of compassion and patience when in conflict with others. Seek more vigorously the distortions and shortcomings in your own vision of things than in those you might seek to overcome. Questions of doctrinal purity, correct theology and behavior, and so on are most helpful in an assessment of oneself before God (on a concrete rather than abstract level), not as a club for bludgeoning others. Much has been forgiven you; you should forgive much in others (see the parable of the unforgiving servant, Matt. 18:21–35).

Such an attitude requires an imaginative ability to stand for a moment in someone else's shoes, a skill few people have or even seem to desire. If a democratic capitalist cannot even imagine why a third-world peasant might be attracted to socialism, or a believer cannot understand why someone else feels they cannot believe; if a secularist cannot even conceive of the vision of a person of faith, then none of them can claim understanding or wisdom. Such people can only be narrow propagandists. They have lost sight of the difficulty everyone faces in making one's way in life. This is not counsel for weak neutrality, but for a compassionate recognition that life is hard, that truth—even if ultimately one—has many faces, that none of us would be exactly who we are if our experiences in life were different.

If we have a love both of truth and of people, we will develop a resistance to knee-jerk responses to particular labels or terminology. A favorite tactic in both subcultures is to forestall thinking by building conditioned responses into a variety of terms so as to evoke immediate, unreflective condemnation or praise. Instant condemnation words for the conservative Christian subculture, for instance, usually include the following: *liberal, existential, relative,* any word starting with *neo-, social* (and its variants), *Communist, pluralism,* and (the current best seller) *humanism.*

Allow me to illustrate this phenomenon at work. I once used Albert Camus's novel, *The Plague,* in an introductory literature class in a conservative Christian college. I intentionally avoided the scare words on the first day of discussion to find what the response of students would be without preconceptions. The discussion went well, and many were clearly interested in learning something of what Camus had to say about the world. As they settled into their seats on the second day, however, a fellow in the front row raised his hand. "My roommate says that Camus is an existentialist. Is that true?" My answer was irrelevant. Nothing more needed to be said. The alarm had been sounded. The mere evocation of the word *existentialist* was sufficient, and I detected a physical change in their faces and posture as their minds shut tight against anything Albert Camus might have to say about the human condition. And do not think this happens, as the stereotype would have us believe, only among narrow-minded conservatives, especially religious ones. The secularist intellectuals are no different, only perhaps slightly more polished.

While the reflective Christian will have some of the same problems with both subcultures, other problems are more likely in relation to one than the other. In the secular, intellectual world, for instance, the believer will often be made to feel guilty or incompetent (the intellectual equivalent of guilty) for operating out of a theistic point of view. By so doing, it is implied, one has forfeited objectivity, reasonableness, balance, and, thereby, respect.

The reflective person need not apologize, however, for having a position, a point of view, or a way of seeing things. It is impossible not to have one, as many secular thinkers are the first to point out. What is really irritating about a Christian world view to many secularists is that it makes unfashionable kinds of truth-claims. It is not so much the content of the claims as the suggestion that if Christian claims are true, then many others are not. This violates, as we have seen, sacred tenets of secular orthodoxy and is not to be tolerated.

Given all my talk about uncertainty and risk, am I not one of those who devalues the notion of truth? Not at all. One does not aid the cause of truth by misrepresenting its nature. Truth is best served, in my view, by our being equally unimpressed with those who claim to have it all, neatly tied in their own package, and with those who peddle the self-fulfilling cliché that there is no truth. Most people who live in the real world understand the foolishness of both.

The susceptibility of both subcultures to trendiness underscores the importance of the reflective Christian not being intimidated into conformity. He or she need not apologize for refusing to jump on every intellectual or spiritual bandwagon that parades down the road. The fads change in these things as quickly as clothing styles, particularly in our century. Fill your closet with the latest "broad-lapel" ideas in modern psychology or Christian evangelism, and you will soon notice that "narrow-lapel" ideas are the coming rage.

I am not suggesting sticking your head in the sand. One should take seriously anything that is shaping the lives and thinking of many people at any given time. One should wrestle with the most recent thought to find what is of value as well as what is influential. Great truths wait still to be discovered, or rediscovered, even if illusion and falsehood are in their heyday. But do not be overly taken with every idea or trend that comes along. Human history is long, and ideas sweep on and off the stage endlessly. The secular faith in endless progress in the nineteenth century gives way to twentieth-century pessimism, the hundred-year rule of nonrepresentation in painting is threatened as the human figure and the landscape creep back onto the canvases of respected painters.

How sad to have one's eternal relationship with God threatened by ways of thinking which may not even last a decade, much less a generation. Ironically, the secular concepts most antagonistic to faith usually fade under *secular* attack, as their inadequacy becomes ever more apparent, not because Christians object to them.

This does not mean that we should simply cling tightly to nineteenth-century formulations of the Christian faith. We are responsible to work out our salvation in our time, in the midst of our culture, not in some other time or place. But it does suggest that we need not be overly dazzled by the bright lights of high-powered secular intellectualism. Flannery O'Connor advocates the cultivation of Christian skepticism as a protection against naive acceptance of everything that threatens faith: "What kept me a sceptic in college was precisely my Christian faith. It always said: wait, don't bite on this, get a wider picture, continue to read." [4]

There is a strange ebb and flow to the intensity of doubt and to the challenges that the heart and mind raise. At certain points in my life I have felt keenly the force of some questions that now do not seem particularly important to me. They were not so much "answered" as they simply moved to the periphery as I grew and changed.

Among the things one should be skeptical about is skepticism itself, particularly in its common secular form and as it edges toward cynicism. Skepticism is the ruling methodology of our day and has been for hundreds of years in Western culture. Peter Elbow calls it "the doubting game" and points out that its two primary strategies are to remove the self from the evaluation process and to end up with truth by focusing on error.[5] Among the many problems of the doubting game is that the obsession with error, like the obsession of Nathaniel Hawthorne's Puritans with evil, encourages one to see it everywhere, making truth just as susceptible to destruction as error itself.

The doubting game also tends to exaggerate the importance of the error-finding faculties—reason, analysis—at the expense of other faculties such as imagination, empathy, synthesis. It underestimates the extent to which reason (and the whole doubting methodology) can *produce* error as well as detect it. It can, even at its best, retard progress toward many important kinds of truth which are not compatible with the doubting game (for example, aesthetic, interpersonal, and spiritual).

Perhaps most damaging of all, thorough skepticism discourages risk-taking. The person playing the doubting game is very afraid of looking foolish, of not appearing logical, rigorous, and disciplined. The obsession with error makes one fear commitment to anything that is not self-evident, or at least embraced by a large percentage of others who play the same game. And what could be more risky than to make assertions about value, about right and wrong, about God, especially if one acts on those assertions?

The secular world of ideas plays the doubting game almost exclusively and is usually scornful of anyone who doesn't. Ironically, however, the church also plays this game to a great extent. The mystery of the gospel, the paradox of the incarnation, the wondrous enigma of grace are freeze-dried into a highly rationalized and/or authoritarian system of theologies, codes, rules, prescriptions, orders of service, and forms of church government. Everything is written down, everything is organized, so that all can be certain and those in error detected.

I am not advocating irrationalism, obscurantism, sloppy thinking, or sappy emotionalism. I am merely suggesting that among the things one should be skeptical about in our skeptical age is the unchallenged primacy of this way of ascertaining truth. It must be balanced by other ways of knowing which employ faculties at least as powerful as reason and which encourage risk and adventure.

One benefit of release from the monopoly of the doubting game is the awareness that a belief, feeling, intuition, or conviction does not have to be "defendable" to be worthwhile. Solzhenitsyn says, "Not everything has a name." [6] Likewise, not everything is explainable. Not everything can be put in terms that allow it to be ground through the doubting-game machine. Even the concepts of "explanation," "defense," and "proof" are derived from one particular way of looking at the world which, while powerful and historically productive, has no valid claim to exclusive rule. Again, this is not an apology for anti-intellectualism or irrationalism, but a recognition that the search for truth is too important to limit ourselves to one faculty or one methodology.

The upshot of all this is that the reflective Christian should not allow his affinity for the life of the mind to blind him or her to the clear shortcomings of the secular, intellectual world, many of which are evident to those with no interest in spiritual things. Do not be intimidated into adopting uncritically a system of thought that, while tremendously useful in many contexts, is also greatly limited in many others, most especially in areas of ultimate significance. Be at least as skeptical of the world of doubting as it is of the world of faith, not out of fear for faith but out of regard for truth.

Abstractions aside, there are very practical guidelines to keep in mind as one tries to work out a productive life in the midst of these two worlds. One of the most important is conservation of energy. Nothing is easier and more futile than being continually entangled in unwinnable and unproductive struggles in either the church or the secular arena. Some battles are necessary and to avoid them is to evade responsibility. Often, however, they are bottomless pits of controversy into which one can pour endless energy better used in other tasks.

This is especially the case since most arguments are not actually over the announced issues but over underlying ones which are unstated, usually unrecognized, and probably more emotional or instinctive than rational. In the conservative Christian subculture, for instance, defending a particular view of Scripture will take on similar proportions to saving Europe in the Middle Ages by stopping the Moslem hordes at Vienna.

It is not a time to seriously consider whether one's position is correct, though there may be a show of concern for logical argument; it is a time to defend one's life and way of life. It's God versus the infidels, light versus dark, the U.S. hockey team against the Russians. It is naive to think you can instantly change someone's outlook in such a situation. So much more is felt to be at stake, consciously or unconsciously, than a point of theology. The same is true with any sacrosanct value of the secular, intellectual subculture. Recognizing this phenomenon will not help you win arguments but can help conserve energy for more useful tasks.

And useful, positive tasks are what the reflective Christian should seek. We live in a contentious age in which people often rally around what they are against. A trivial but symbolic example is a group whose name is something like "Partners Free from Children," who apparently get together to celebrate their right as couples not to have children. They inspire me to contemplate starting a club called "People Who Don't Own Corvettes," but I doubt there is a place big enough for us all to meet.

We should avoid being sucked into negative struggles that are characterized primarily by what they are against, depending often on fear, suspicion, and even hatred for their primary motivation. Seek out, instead, constructive tasks that bring healing, enlightenment, and encouragement rather than bitterness and enmity. Organize meetings against abortion clinics if that is what you feel God asks of you, but organize two more for aiding unwed mothers and single parents. Criticize the church when such criticism is called for, but also seek ways with your own life to make it what it should be. And aside from controversial things, there should be paintings painted, plays performed, poems written, discoveries made, ideas explored, causes pursued, and tasks accomplished which have nothing to do with partisanship of any kind, simply because we are human beings whom God has given many, many things to do.

And while you are engaged in these tasks, it is best, if you have any potential for it at all, to develop and exercise a sense of humor. God gave us laughter to relieve the strain of living in a fallen world. It is particularly useful in dealing with the gap between expectation and reality, pronouncement and action that characterizes hypocrisy. Kierkegaard saw hypocrisy as essentially comic, as is the person who forgets that he or she is a finite, existing individual rather than a detached apologist, saint, or thinking machine.

Humor can assuage the tension of paradox, the pain of uncertainty and insecurity, the fear of the future. Correctly used, it helps us keep things in perspective, see ourselves honestly, accept the limits of the human condition. It can defuse debilitating anger without undercutting our resolve to see right triumph. Like everything else humor can be misused to hurt and destroy, but it can also help us be healers and reconcilers in a troubled world.

*   *   *   *   *

It had not been Alex's intention to talk to anyone about it, least of all to Sarah Lawrence. How do you talk about something so indefinite anyway? How do you begin to say that somehow life seems heavy, that you find your energy sapped when you haven't even been working hard, that cynicism has become a reflexive response, that every human activity seems strangely pointless?

And with Sarah Lawrence, a woman nearing the end of a long but hardly distinguished teaching career? She was a member of his department, but he hadn't seen much of her. Actually, it was sort of embarrassing. He was new at Redeemed and she had been teaching when he was born, yet they had made him chairman of the department on his arrival.

He had liked what little he knew of her, but had not been drawn to know more. She had a reputation as a dry teacher, one who told students much more about Sir Philip Sydney than any of them wanted to know. And yet he had heard that students would come to her with things they would not tell anyone else in the world.

Still, she was hardly the one he would have sought out

had he been looking for help, and he wasn't looking. Help, however, found him in the faculty lounge. It was actually too generous to call it a lounge, being more like a storage room with a coffee pot. The President did not believe in coddling the faculty. It made them expect raises, respect, and other foolishness.

Sarah initiated the conversation as she filled her cup at the coffee pot. "You're looking a little worn, Alex—and this is only October. How are you going to make it to June?"

"I don't know that I am."

"That bad, huh?"

"Worse."

"Don't let them get you down, Alex."

How much did she know? How did she know?

She read the quizzical look on his face. "Don't worry. Nobody's been talking. I just know how things work around here, and I've seen people like you come and go over the years. I have to admit I laughed right out loud when I started reading that article of yours responding to Shell's view of existentialism. 'Oh this poor boy,' I said to myself, 'he knows not what he does.' "

"I sure didn't, and I still don't. Explain these people to me, Sarah. I don't understand them."

"They're sinners."

"Please, none of that. Everything around here is packaged in that maddening Christian jargon. It's enough to make one long for simple idol worship."

"All right, let's just say they're human beings then."

"What does that explain?"

"Everything. They're like everyone else—trying to survive, trying to make sense out of things, trying to find a reason for getting up in the morning."

"But they're narrow, two-faced, hypocritical, judgmental. . . ."

Sarah interrupted him and continued the list, ". . . self-righteous, sometimes arrogant, often foolish—like I said, human beings."

"But they don't see themselves that way at all. They think they're God's gift to the world."

"They are. They're both. God works with what He's got. Besides, they aren't nearly as self-satisfied as they seem. Privately, most of them feel as tentative about themselves as you do. They've just been taught they must have the answer to everything, and that's quite a burden. They're really good people at the bottom of it all."

"That's easy enough for you to say. You haven't been burned the way I have."

Sarah smiled sadly and paused a moment. Alex wanted to retrieve his statement, but she spoke first.

"Haven't I been a believer for almost fifty years?"

"Yes, listen, I didn't mean. . . ."

She went on as though speaking to herself words she had never said out loud before.

"Don't I know the shortcomings of God's people? Haven't I seen every kind of manipulation of Scripture? Haven't I witnessed all the uses and abuses of authority, legitimate and illegitimate, known to man? Don't I know the sting of gifts denied, of doors closed, of common prejudice and ignorance dressed in the cloak of spirituality?

"Let me tell you just a little bit about my past, and we'll let that little bit stand for everything else. When I was a young girl, I had a love for Jesus that I've never quite matched since. He was so clearly everything I wanted to be—not just good, but a force for good. I didn't want to just be good, I wanted to do righteousness—like Jesus did when He healed the sick and cast out demons. I looked at my own little world and at the bigger one beyond and said, 'Sarah, there's casting out to be done here and you and Jesus are going to do it.'

"I loved Jesus for hating evil and sickness and death, and I tried to hate them too the way He did. When I saw boys at school being mean to someone, I'd try in my mind to bind them in Jesus' name, and sometimes I thought it worked.

"One day the pastor was visiting and everyone was sitting around smiling and feeling uncomfortable. To break one of

the dry spells the pastor asked my little brother, 'And what
are you going to be when you grow up, son?' And I didn't
even hear what my brother said because I was trying to think
what I was going to say when he asked me. But, you know,
he didn't ask me. I was sitting there on that footrest right
next to my brother, who was barely old enough to talk, but
he never asked what I was going to do, and they started off
talking about something else.

"I thought he'd just forgotten to ask so I blurted out, 'I'm
going to be a preacher.' My mother let out a little gasp and
my father stretched his neck. I thought for a moment I'd
said a dirty word.

" 'You mean a teacher, dear,' my mother said. But I stuck
to my guns and all my secret dreams came rolling fearfully
out. 'No, a preacher, and maybe a prophet too, and I'm going
to make sick people well, and stop bad men from hurting
folks.' I felt frightened by what I heard myself saying, but
also excited and, by the saying of it, confirmed in what until
that moment I'd never said quite that clearly even to myself.

"There was a brief moment of silence and then the pastor
broke into a laugh. 'Well, that's just great, little darling. That's
a wonderful attitude. Now, Jesus doesn't want you to be a
preacher, but He does want you to serve Him. I think someday
you will make some pastor a wonderful helpmate and the two
of you can serve the Lord together.'

"And I was so relieved that I had gotten off the hook and
that they got down to eating the cookies my mother hurriedly
passed around that it wasn't until later that I felt the disap-
pointment and the hurt. And I did stop thinking that I was
going to be a preacher, and felt a little stupid for ever thinking
that I could have been. And somehow, I'm not sure why, I
started loving Jesus just a little less."

Alex sat for a moment. "Why, Sarah, a closet feminist at
a place like Redeemed?"

"No, I'm not a feminist. They wouldn't have me, and in
many ways I wouldn't have them. But maybe I do understand
what motivates them better than most people around here."

Alex felt suddenly close to someone that ten minutes before had been only the stereotypical old-maid English teacher. He wanted to know more. "But why have you stayed a part of this little corner of the world all these years? Didn't you ever rebel? Haven't you ever wanted to find some other place where you could breathe more freely?"

"Oh, the answers to those questions are long ones. Did I rebel? Yes, in my own way. Why have I stayed? I don't know exactly. Maybe if I were young today I wouldn't. It wasn't so clear years ago that there were other ways of being a believer. Besides, I wouldn't have just been leaving a church or a denomination, I would have been leaving everything I knew. It would have been like giving up breathing because my lungs were congested."

She stopped for a moment, her face concentrated in thought and feeling. "Most important, though, and I don't know if you can understand this, it would have been giving up those people who care about me the most. They are the people who cared enough to patiently teach me all the antiquated traditions, all the sentimental songs, all their silly, little idiosyncrasies, so that I, Sarah Lawrence, could be one of God's people. And, you know, in the midst of all that hodgepodge of fundamentalist faith, and populist politics, and work ethic capitalism, and farmer's almanac science, and midwestern dullness, and other odd pieces of string, I somehow met God. Amongst those people, He first called me by name, and said, 'Sarah, I will be your God, and you will be one of my people.'

"How do you walk away from that, Alex? And where do you walk to? To other people who are just as silly, who simply have a different mix of blind spots and prejudices, but who don't detect on you the family smell? To people who think they are magnanimous by letting you drown doing your own thing, who have no God-hunger, and find your own amusing at best? No, Alex, for me at least there weren't any greener pastures. Or, if there were, they were somewhere inside me."

"That's depressing news, Sarah. I've been living the last couple of months on the belief that there had to be greener pastures somewhere. I can't imagine having to spend a lifetime in this kind of atmosphere. I don't think my faith could take it. How can you listen to these people with the name of God constantly on their lips while leading their mincing little, penny-ante lives, and not feel a drain on your own desire for God?"

Sarah laughed briefly. "I learned a long time ago what and who it was I believe in—and it wasn't my parents or my pastor or old deacon Smithson, who was a bigger gossip than all the women in my childhood church put together. And it certainly wasn't Redeemed College. No, I decided long ago that I was willing to risk a life only on the One who said,

> The Spirit of the Lord God is upon me,
> Because the Lord has anointed me
> To bring good news to the afflicted;
> He has sent me to bind up the broken-hearted,
> To proclaim liberty to captives,
> And freedom to prisoners;
> To proclaim the favorable year of the Lord, . . .
> To comfort all who mourn, . . .

Anything less than that isn't worth the risk."

"But why in the middle of these people? Why not someplace where faith isn't mixed up with quite so many other things? I mean some of these people genuinely believe God is a free-market Republican."

"Why not, indeed. There are of course many other places. This is just one little, back-water spot in the river of faith. But it is the place in which I have been put, and in which I have chosen to stay. Maybe it isn't the place for you. In fact, it probably isn't. But do let me say this. Don't make the mistake of thinking there's another time or another place where following God will come easier. It doesn't work that way, Alex. You have everything you need for your contentment or misery within the confines of your own heart. That will go with you wherever you go. Every place has its pitfalls and absurdities, just as each has its opportunities and measures of grace."

"Maybe I would be better off teaching at a state college or someplace like that."

"Could be. But don't think foolishness resides only within the gates of this college. It is a characteristic of the species. There is certainly a lot of work to be done no matter where you are, and the temptation will always be to do something else instead."

Alex wasn't sure what this last phrase meant, but he had no opportunity to question Sarah about it. The door to the lounge cracked open and the Dean stretched in his neck.

"Ah, a meeting of the English department. You two discussing misplaced modifiers, are you?" He had on his most polyester grin.

"You're half right," Alex responded.

"Just thought I'd let you know it's 10:28. Chapel in two minutes."

Alex looked at Sarah and they both smiled. "Wouldn't miss it, Dean. Wouldn't miss it."

* * * * *

All this sterling advice notwithstanding, the reflective Christian probably should simply get used to the idea of living in partial tension with his or her world. Even practicing the kind of humility, compassion, and empathy I have suggested will be seen by some as signs of weakness. Who wants a leader, for instance, who gives the opposition the benefit of the doubt? How can you inspire people by telling them their cause is a mixture of truth and error? How can you get people to sacrifice (and give money) if you don't make it perfectly clear that all that is good and wholesome is on your side, and all that is evil and despicable is on the other? To the crusader, the moderate is as repugnant as the enemy, for moderation threatens the resolve of the "true believers."

Everyone wants to be liked. We need the affirmation of at least a few that our existence is appreciated. Most do not enjoy conflict; certainly we don't want to be thought dangerous, deluded, a bad influence, foolish, or fallen away. Most will go to great lengths to be accommodating, to explain and even modify themselves so as to fit in. The fear of being cast out is instinctive and visceral. In primitive cultures it literally meant death, and the psychological reality of that has not entirely changed.

In filling these pages with words, some form of this fear has never been far away. What might conservative Christians think of my using Kierkegaard and Barth so much? What would the secular intellectual think of me for even worrying about such a thing? Will people find me threatening or be warned away by institutional defenders? Will I be given a label beginning with *neo-* or ending in *-ist?* Will I be accused of "subtly" or "unknowingly" doing something dastardly, even though my intentions are all the best? Will I be identified with "the slide" toward this or that?

"Who cares?" some would say. "I care," I must respond, especially if, like Pascal, I desire above all that truth not be overcome in my hands. For might not my detractors be right? Might not I be hindering the cause of truth and good with all my ruminations about uncertainty and limitations and risk? Or perhaps, others might say, I haven't gone nearly far enough in that direction. And now I am back where we began, harassed by my powers of reflection to the point of paralysis, and I am reminded that *the pressures on the reflective Christian will always be greater from within than without.*

And as I reach a point of potential paralysis, as I have before and will again, I remind myself of the facts as I know them and the commitments I have made. I am willing to begin once more at the beginning, to rethink and rebelieve from square one, even knowing that this time I may end up not believing at all. God is not afraid or offended by this—He who heard a wail of desperate questioning even from His own Son.

This is not without risk—what of value is? It is no blank check for "whatever-I-feel-like" theologies or world views. Wisdom dictates that I check my way against the experiences, past and present, of fellow believers. But I must also check it against my own mind and heart—for I have only my own, not someone else's, or that of some other age. I can finally affirm only what lives for me, at this point in time and space, in the interstices of my soul. What falls away is not necessarily chaff; but what remains, God willing, will be what is required for the work I am called to do in God's working out of His will for His creation.

I have learned to live with the rise and fall of the thoughts and feelings of faith, to co-exist with honest doubt, to accept tension and paradox without clinging to it as an excuse for inaction. I have learned to be a minority without seeking to be an adversary. I am trying to do what people of faith have always done—respond to revelation by my own best lights, struggle to understand all that can be understood and have reverence for the rest, act beyond my certain knowledge in the faith that such action is blessed. "Lord, I believe; help thou my unbelief."

Epilogue

Something to Live and Die For

...the movement of faith is unceasing, because no explanation it offers is ever finished.
—*Jacques Ellul*

"Meaning" is the most stirring of all spiritual impulses....
—*Helmut Thielicke*

THE MOST IMPORTANT AND DESIRABLE things in the human experience have no physical existence. One of these is "meaning." What is meaning? Why do we want it? How do we get it? Is it an actual quality in reality to be discerned, or something we project upon that reality from within, or only a never-to-be-fulfilled longing of the human heart?

Whatever it is, it offers one of the most powerful reasons for continuing the human experiment. Its possibility is, simply, a reason to live—its absence, a reason to give up living. Our appetite for meaning is insatiable, our anxiety over its elusiveness never ending. The response to this fundamental human desire is as varied as are human beings themselves. People reach out for meaning in an endless number of ways, often mistaking the diversions of life for meaning itself.

No one feels this desire for meaning more strongly than the reflective man or woman. If one has meaning in life, then any circumstance is bearable; if not, then none is. (How is it that Mother Teresa can say that many affluent Westerners are more to be pitied than the poorest of the poor whom she serves? Are there worse things than not having a roof over your head?)

The problem of meaning is tied directly to that of transience. We haven't much time to figure things out. I am keenly aware of the brevity of my life. I don't know why this is. It is a perception I have had since late childhood, long before I read any "carpe diem" poetry. This perception has been sharpened by the modest amount of traveling I have done abroad. Every English churchyard, every monument, every initial carved in a dungeon stone testifies to my own transience. What does it matter that this chap lived from 1612 until 1648? He died when only thirty-six, but what if he had lived to be eighty-six? He still would have been dead for three hundred years either way. And what does it matter how long I live, or what I do, when one considers the long stretch of human history (or, on a cosmic scale, its brief flicker)?

It only matters if meaning is, in fact, possible for my life, for every human life. I return once more to Kierkegaard. An entry in his journal expresses for me the ultimate goal of my temporal existence and speaks for many people of faith from all ages: "The thing is to understand myself, to see what God wishes *me* to do; the thing is to find a truth which is true *for me,* to find *the idea for which I can live and die*" (his emphasis).[1] To find an idea, a cause, a purpose around which I can construct a life; to realize that such a purpose also allows one to come to terms with the end of life—what could be more desirable?

Where is one to find such an idea? Kierkegaard—like Abraham, Gideon, Rahab, Peter, Augustine, Pascal, Solzhenitsyn, and a long line in my own family—found it in God. He took the risk that this was something worth the spending of a life, the only one he would ever have to spend. But he realized it was only so if this truth were personal and integrated into the messy details of his own life: "What would be the use of discovering so-called objective truth, of working through all the systems of philosophy . . . ;—what good would it do me to be able to explain the meaning of Christianity if it had *no* deeper significance *for me and for my life* . . . ?"[2]

This is not egotistic self-indulgence, but the recognition that we each exist as unique creations before God, working out our own lives by our best lights, and that what does not exist in *my* life does not, for me at least, exist at all. And something as voracious as faith in God must permeate the whole of my being, not simply reside in the clinical theater of my reason or in the fluctuating tide of my emotions.

Having something to live and die for implies a life of action. It suggests there are things worth doing. It commends the exercise of the will to throw off the paralysis of uncertainty and indecision so that we may join with others and with God in making meaningful the human experiment. It calls up words like involvement, risk, and commitment—words not in keeping with the temper of our times.

And no one can predict where these words might take us. There is no prescription for what a committed life must look like. It will of necessity find different people doing greatly different things. Commitment will not necessarily lead to "big" things, God's own interest being so often in the seemingly trivial and mundane. It will often entangle us with other human beings, the only earthly things which last forever.

Commitment will not guarantee one feeling at home in the world, or in the subcultures in which we find ourselves—and if at home, only rarely at ease. Commitment inevitably draws resistance—from those whose commitments are different and from those who resent any commitment at all. And what of the inner resistance of one's own uncertainties and fears, a force beside which all the others often pale?

Overcoming these resistances requires an unusual balance of self-confidence, humility, and integrity. It requires holding tightly to the value of the struggle, while holding loosely the conclusions we draw while in the midst. It calls for discerning between the opposition which must be overcome and that which calls us to a higher standard. We need to forgive as we are forgiven. We should pursue God tenaciously; we should neither exaggerate our knowledge of His ways, which are not our ways, nor ignore the benefits of His grace which are offered us at every moment.

Pascal observed that faith is suited to all kinds of minds. The particular kind of faith I have tried to describe is not necessarily the most desirable. It is one way of believing in the modern world, one which is as old, however, as the world itself. As God truly rewards those who seek Him, it is a way which He blesses.

Notes

Introduction

Epigraph
Karl Barth, "The Need and Promise of Christian Preaching," in *The Word of God and the Word of Man*, trans. Douglas Horton (Gloucester, Mass.: Peter Smith, 1978), pp. 125–26.

1. Blaise Pascal, *Penseés* (New York: E. P. Dutton, 1958), p. 198.

Chapter 1
THE NATURE OF REFLECTION

Epigraph
T. S. Eliot, "Ash-Wednesday," in *The Complete Poems and Plays, 1909–1950* (New York: Harcourt, Brace, and World, 1962), p. 61.

1. From *The Poems of Gerard Manley Hopkins*, 4th ed. (1918; rpt. New York: Oxford U. P., 1967), pp. 102–03.
2. Flannery O'Connor, *The Habit of Being*, ed. Sally Fitzgerald (New York: Farrar, Straus, Giroux, 1979), p. 131.
3. Soren Kierkegaard, *The Point of View of My Work As an Author*, in *The Modern Tradition: Backgrounds of Modern Literature*, ed. Richard Ellmann and Charles Feidelson, Jr., (New York: Oxford U. P., 1965), p. 751.
4. Jacques Ellul, *Living Faith: Belief and Doubt in a Perilous World*, trans. Peter Heinegg (New York: Harper and Row, 1980), p. 230.

Chapter 2
THE REFLECTIVE CHRISTIAN AND THE CHURCH

Epigraphs
Blaise Pascal, *Penseés* (New York: E. P. Dutton, 1958), p. 265.

From a Lenny Bruce comedy routine.

1. Jacques Ellul, *Living Faith: Belief and Doubt in a Perilous World*, trans. Peter Heinegg (New York: Harper and Row, 1980), p. 109.
2. Flannery O'Connor, *The Habit of Being*, ed. Sally Fitzgerald (New York: Farrar, Straus, Giroux, 1979), pp. 93, 227.
3. Karl Barth, "The Need and Promise of Christian Preaching," in *The Word of God and the Word of Man*, trans. Douglas Horton (Gloucester, Mass.: Peter Smith, 1978), pp. 130–31.

Chapter 3
THE REFLECTIVE CHRISTIAN IN THE SECULAR WORLD

Epigraphs
Flannery O'Connor, *The Habit of Being,* ed. Sally Fitzgerald (New York: Farrar, Straus, Giroux, 1979), p. 231.

Soren Kierkegaard, *Philosophical Fragments,* in *A Kierkegaard Anthology,* ed. Robert Bretall (Princeton: Princeton U. P., 1946), p. 167.

Matthew 11:6.

1. See "Religion and Literature," in T. S. Eliot, *Selected Essays* (New York: Harcourt, Brace, and World, 1964), p. 352.

Chapter 4
THE SEARCH FOR TRUTH AND CERTAINTY

Epigraphs
Blaise Pascal, *Penseés* (New York: E. P. Dutton, 1958), p. 64.

Soren Kierkegaard, *Concluding Unscientific Postscript* in *A Kierkegaard Anthology,* ed. Robert Bretall (Princeton: Princeton U. P., 1946), p. 222.

1. T. S. Eliot, Introduction to *Penseés* (New York: E. P. Dutton, 1958), p. xv. (This essay also found in Eliot's *Selected Essays.*)
2. Blaise Pascal, *Penseés,* pp. 19–20.

Chapter 5
THE RISK OF COMMITMENT

Epigraphs
Blaise Pascal, *Penseés* (New York: E. P. Dutton, 1958), p. 77.

Soren Kierkegaard, *The Journals,* in *A Kierkegaard Anthology,* ed. Robert Bretall (Princeton: Princeton U. P. 1946), p. 281.

Helmut Thielicke, *Between Heaven and Earth: Conversations with American Christians,* trans. John W. Doberstein (New York: Harper and Row, 1965), p. 103.

1. Henri Bergson, *Creative Evolution,* in *The Modern Tradition: Backgrounds of Modern Literature,* ed. Richard Ellmann and Charles Feidelson, Jr., (New York: Oxford U. P., 1965), p. 725.
2. Alexander Solzhenitsyn, *Nobel Lecture,* trans. F. D. Reeve (New York: Farrar, Straus, Giroux, 1972), pp. 19–20.

3. Flannery O'Connor, *The Habit of Being,* ed. Sally Fitzgerald (New York: Farrar, Straus, Giroux, 1979), p. 90.

4. Robert McAfee Brown, *Is Faith Obsolete?* (Philadelphia: Westminster Press, 1974), pp. 142 ff.

5. Ibid., p. 144.

6. Henri Nouwen, *The Genesee Diary: Report from a Trappist Monastery* (Garden City, N.Y.: Doubleday, 1976), p. 40.

7. Karl Barth, "The Gift of Freedom: Foundation of Evangelical Ethics," trans. Thomas Weiser in *The Humanity of God* (Richmond, Va.: John Knox Press, 1964), p. 79.

8. Flannery O'Connor, *The Habit of Being,* p. 223.

9. Blaise Pascal, *Penseés,* p. 76.

10. Karl Barth, "The Gift of Freedom," p. 72.

11. Flannery O'Connor, *The Habit of Being,* p. 97.

12. Helmut Thielicke, *Nihilism: Its Origin and Nature—with a Christian Answer,* trans. John W. Doberstein (New York: Schocken Books, 1969), p. 161.

13. See "Baudelaire," in T. S. Eliot, *Selected Essays* (New York: Harcourt, Brace, and World, 1964), pp. 371–81.

14. Soren Kierkegaard, *Concluding Unscientific Postscript,* in *A Kierkegaard Anthology,* p. 250.

15. Ibid., p. 107.

Chapter 6
SURVIVING AS A REFLECTIVE CHRISTIAN

Epigraphs
Soren Kierkegaard, *The Attack Upon "Christendom"* in *A Kierkegaard Anthology,* ed. Robert Bretall (Princeton: Princeton U. P., 1946), p. 445.

Karl Barth, "The Need and Promise of Christian Preaching," in *The Word of God and the Word of Man,* trans. Douglas Horton (Gloucester, Mass.: Peter Smith, 1978), p. 129.

1. Blaise Pascal, *Penseés* (New York: E. P. Dutton, 1958), p. 271.

2. Soren Kierkegaard, *The Sickness Unto Death,* in *A Kierkegaard Anthology* p. 345.

3. Simone Weil, quoted in Helmut Thielicke, *Faith Letters,* trans. Douglas Crow (Waco, Texas: Word, 1978), p. 11.

4. Flannery O'Connor, *The Habit of Being,* ed. Sally Fitzgerald (New York: Farrar, Straus, Giroux, 1979), pp. 477–78.

5. Peter Elbow, "The Doubting Game and the Believing Game—An Analysis of the Intellectual Enterprise," in *Writing Without Teachers* (New York: Oxford U. P., 1973), pp. 147–91.

6. Alexander Solzhenitsyn, *Nobel Lecture,* trans. F. D. Reeve (New York: Farrar, Straus, Giroux, 1972), p. 5.

Epilogue
SOMETHING TO LIVE AND DIE FOR

Epigraph
Jacques Ellul, *Living Faith: Belief and Doubt in a Perilous World,* trans.
Peter Heinegg (New York: Harper and Row, 1980), p. 268.

Helmut Thielicke, *Nihilism: Its Origin and Nature—with a Christian Answer,*
trans. John W. Doberstein (New York: Schocken Books, 1969), p. 31.

1. Soren Kierkegaard, *The Journals,* in *A Kierkegaard Anthology,* ed.
Robert Bretall (Princeton: Princeton U. P., 1946), p. 5.

2. Ibid.